TESTIMONIALS ON THE FINAL PUSH

Going into final year of University, Dela had an average of 38%. After successfully using the strategies in The Final Push, he achieved the impossible and graduated with a **Second-Class Honours Upper Division (2:1) degree.**

"Well I guess coming from a Ghanaian background, it was really important to do well because I felt I had a lot of expectations, and especially as my mum sacrificed a lot to send me to a good school so...I felt I needed to try and achieve the best.

The main thing Mayo talked about was your change in habits and approach and how that helped you, and honestly for the majority of students in your/our position, they already have the "brains" to do it, they most likely lack either motivation or the little extra in terms of technique to get them over the line."

-Dela
University of Manchester,
Second-Class Honours Upper Division (2:1), Bsc Economics

"This book is definitely what everyone needs to get their life on the right track; both University students and those who are struggling to reach their goals. I like the fact that the book encourages you to tell yourself the hard truth and also to dream vividly and to take precise steps to make that dream and those feelings you dream about a reality...great book!"

-Yimika
University of Loughborough,
Second-Class Honours Upper Division (2:1),
Bachelor of Arts (BA), International Relations and Affairs

"I just graduated from University. However, this book is relevant to anyone who is struggling to achieve their dreams. I love the fact that the writer gives his own personal experience, it is an easy read and the story is told smoothly. I'll recommend this to anyone."

-Ife
Profession: Management Consultant
University of Nottingham,
Second-Class Honours Upper Division (2:1),
Bachelor of Science (BSc), Finance, Accounting and
Management

"One of the main techniques which made the biggest difference was doing work every single day and working from the beginning so that by the end you are just revising and practising exam questions.

I have personally spent three years improving my grades from my poor performance with A Levels, and the techniques Mayo has suggested is exactly what I have been using to discover how to get first class marks. The most important thing is that it all comes down to technique and strategy."

– Jaspreet
University Degree: University of Hertfordshire, First Class
Honours in Biological Sciences

THE FINAL PUSH

THE FINAL PUSH

A Short Inspirational Step-by-Step Guide on How To Get First Class Marks

MAYO OSHIN

Published by
Mayo Oshin

First Published: 2015

ISBN: 978 978 946 486 9

DEDICATION

This book is dedicated to:
My family, particularly Wole and Titi (Mum & Dad), for supporting me consistently all these years and giving me the foundation to succeed in life. Your time, energy, and money have not gone to waste.

My brother from another mother, Nigel, my right hand man through all the most memorable moments in University.

My final year coach, mentor, and inspiration: Olga. Thank you for opening my mind to what was possible and dedicating many hours to helping me through my final year.

Finally, my University lecturers and tutors. Though you doubted my dream, you were still willing to put up with my annoying questions and support me during office hours.

CONTENTS

PART 1: THE FUNDAMENTALS

PART 2: THE EXTRAS
STUDY ESSENTIALS AND STRATEGIES

PART 3: APPENDIX

PREFACE

Why did I write this book?

I never thought I'd ever write a book and put myself out there like this, but someone had to do it.

Going into my final year of University, I had searched online for anything from somebody who would understand my situation, inspire me to achieve my dream graduation degree, and provide simple practical steps at the same time.

Unfortunately, most of what I read online was generic and broad information: "5 tips to study better", "10 better ways to take notes", or "how to sleep better in your final year". Yes, these were interesting to read, but they weren't exactly what I needed at that time. The impossible was staring me in the face, and I needed real life practical inspiration.

Following my graduation and countless interactions with final-year students, I quickly realized that a lot more final-year students than I had ever imagined expressed a similar need and frustration. They were also looking for real life inspirational and practical examples on how they could achieve first class marks turn their graduation dreams into reality.

This became much clearer to me after I had posted my success story on online student forums. Unexpectedly, I began to receive a lot of positive feedback, requests for mentorship, coaching, and support. What followed over the following two years was remarkable.

Several of these students, who I had inspired and supported, went on to achieve their dream university degrees on graduation day.

I have pulled together everything I have learned from my university experiences, as well as from other successful students, into this book.

My purpose for writing this book is simply to:

Inspire you to believe that whatever graduation dream you have in mind is possible, and share with you simple, practical steps so that you can take action right now to make it a reality.

WHAT TO EXPECT FROM THIS BOOK AND HOW IT'S STRUCTURED

First off, this book is not a magic bullet. If you happen to have found this book close to the end of your final year and haven't yet done any work during the year, don't expect much to come out of it.

Also, if you're not willing to take action on the information in this book, then you can't really complain if you don't get the results you want.

What I can guarantee is that if you are willing to put in the work, take responsibility for where you are now, and take action on what you read in this book, your odds of graduating with the degree you desire will increase significantly.

The structure and content of this book is straightforward. Part 1 contains the main content of the book and covers the fundamentals and essential ingredients you need to maximise your marks and achieve first class marks. This part is broken down into three sections, and I will be taking you through a simple recommended step-by-step process from start to finish.

Throughout this book, I will also be using my "real life" experiences (you will see these in quotation marks) in the context of the different steps explained. This way, you will see real life examples of how you can apply the ideas I introduce.

To help you learn and digest the information better, I've included end of chapter summaries, lessons, and recaps in the book.

In Part 2, you will find 'bonus' content focused on providing specific solutions to common problems you may face during the semester. This includes information on how to overcome procrastination, lack of motivation, how to take better notes, write first class essays and more.

At the end of this book you will find a worksheet to further support you towards your goals.

The three main sections in Part 1 are summarized below:

Section I

This part covers the pre-requisite recommended steps you should take towards your dream. I dish out some tough love here about excuses and self-belief issues, so brace yourself.

The key point is that you must make a personal decision to take complete responsibility for where you are right now and where you will end up at the end of your final year.

I also talk about the power of having a clear vision of your goal and how you can effectively create a vision that you strongly and emotionally connect with in your mind. This part is a crucial foundation before moving on to the rest of the book. Your vision will be your source of motivation to achieve your goals.

Section II

Here, I go deeper into what success looks like and the exact steps you can take to replicate this for yourself. There's no point trying to reinvent the wheel when there is already a formula of what works.

We will take a look at the 4 habits of highly successful students and how you can adopt these to achieve the success you desire. You will learn how to give examiners exactly what they want so that you can get high scores, how to manage your time effectively and stop procrastinating, and how to further increase your chances of success by building the right social network.

Finally, you will learn how to stay motivated and be full of energy throughout the year without burnout and also how to have peace of mind and avoid panic and anxiety.

Section III

In this final part, I talk about those crucial last of months or days towards the end of the year, as well as important deadlines. This period is no joke, and many students crumble at this point, but we can, and will, finish strong.

I will show you two radical, unconventional solutions to the common problems of PADS (Panic Anxiety Depression and Stress) that you may face in this period. Then, I'll talk about exam and revision strategies to make sure that your hard work doesn't go to waste.

How to use this book

Most likely, you are already applying some of the ideas and steps I introduce in this book. That's great! It's also possible you aren't applying some of these steps and ideas. As you read, the key is to try and understand 'why' the different concepts and ideas work. By understanding why it works, you can create your own strategies of achieving your academic goals.

I also recommend you read through the entire book. This way you have better clarity of what you are already doing now that will contribute to your desired goal, what you should stop doing, and what you need to introduce to your life.

Afterwards, you can always come back to the book as a reference for inspiration through tough times and focus on sections of the book that address your specific weak points.

Finally, make use of the bonus (free material) at the end of the book. These will really help you simplify all the information you have read into real practical steps and follow through successfully.

What does success mean to you?

You may feel that a second-class honours degree on graduation day is a very satisfactory and successful achievement. Maybe that dream of graduating with a first-class honours degree is all you can think about and desire.

Allow me to define success for the purpose of this book.

Success is all about giving everything you have to achieve your dream, without compromising your integrity, health, and sanity. This may sound a bit insensitive, but your graduation degree does not define your self-worth nor your success in life. You may not understand this now, but later, it will all make sense.

This is why I have constructed this book; so that you can achieve your graduation dreams without having to lose your life and health in the process. This should be an enjoyable journey that you will remember for years to come.

TERMINOLOGY

If you happen to be a student who is not based in the UK, the university degree lingo you will come across is explained below:

First-class degree, a.k.a. 1st: This is the highest possible undergraduate degree and mark achieved by attaining an overall mark of 70% or higher in a university in the United Kingdom.

Second-class honours, upper division, a.k.a. 2:1: Marks ranging from 60%-69%

Second-class honours, lower division, a.k.a. 2:2: Marks ranging from 50%-59%

Third-class honours, a.k.a. 3rd: This is the lowest recognized undergraduate degree in the United Kingdom. Marks ranging from 40%-49%. This is the range I was in, prior to going into my final year of University.

PART 1
THE FUNDAMENTALS

INTRODUCTION

It's 9 am in the morning, the weather outside isn't looking great, and I already had a feeling I had to prepare for the worst. I had already had breakfast and spent 2 hours in the gym to try and get my anxiety to die down. I was honestly fearful of my results.

No, these weren't my final year graduation results; this was the year before that. All the partying and "living for the moment" in the previous semester seemed very distant, and at that point, I regretted it all. I had spent more time working out and socializing than I had spent studying for all my exam units combined.

I couldn't run away any longer. My parents were waiting downstairs to hear from me. I took a deep breath, opened my laptop, and quickly logged into my student portal to get my results. I didn't expect the results to flash that quickly in my face. They did, and I felt like I got stabbed in the chest.

I had averaged a borderline **third class,** and this time I had to take full responsibility. I had no excuses, nowhere to run, and no plan of action.

I was in a state of shock and so were my parents. Averaging first class marks in my final year seemed like an impossible feat. So what do I do next?

What do you do when your dream seems so far out of your current reality that you don't even know what first step to take? I had no clue what that kind of success would look like, what habits would help, what lifestyle I should cultivate and what mind-set I should have. I felt like I was in the middle of a desert with no compass to escape.

Stranded!

Surely, somebody would believe that it was possible to attain that dream. Unfortunately, this wasn't the case.

I approached my University tutor at the start of the year for help. I asked, "Sir, how can I achieve a first class average mark this year?" After a quick glance at my previous years' marks, he quickly noted I had never even had a single first class mark in any module. He told me it was a feat he believed was very unlikely, and he couldn't remember the last time such a large jump in marks had happened.

I spoke to some other lecturers, and they all said the same thing. I was deflated, and my mind went blank. I had no more thoughts, no more ideas, but also no more excuses.

How on earth was I going to get a First?!

Nobody believed I could pull it off, neither my parents, nor my friends, lecturers, and tutor. **Nobody**!

I knelt down in my room and honestly prayed to God for the first time in years, "God please, I need your help right now. I have no one else around me who understands the situation I am in right now. Please help me!"

From that moment forward, I had this inexplicable peace of mind and a sense of divine guidance.

GAME ON!

SECTION I

THE FIRST STEPS TO SUCCESS

"Faith is taking the first step even when you don't see the whole staircase."

-Martin Luther King, Jr.

STEP 1

TAKE RESPONSIBILITY FOR YOUR CURRENT AND FUTURE SITUATIONS

I'm going to dish out some tough love. I hope you're ready.

On graduation day there is only one person responsible for that degree. You!

Nobody cares about the fact that you messed up your exam results in the previous year because you didn't know how to study. Nobody cares that you're breaking up with your long-term boyfriend, or that your girlfriend messed you up mentally and affected your results, or dare I say, a close relative dies.

I'm sorry.

Nobody cares about your excuses, valid or otherwise. In this cruel world, we only care about results, and success is the only universal language people understand and follow.

All that work from the beginning of your educational experience, from pre-school to high school and now college, has come to a conclusion.

How will you be remembered and what mark will you leave?

Your university degree will stay with you for the rest of your life.

If you're in a tricky situation similar to the one I was in, I strongly advise you to get rid of the silly excuses: "My lecturer tricked me in the exam", "I don't enjoy my course", or "There are too many essay deadlines."

Please stop all of this now for your own sake!

This is the final push, and your success is now completely in your own hands. Take responsibility for the current marks you have as you go into final year, and most importantly, the actions you are going to take every single day to make your dream university degree a reality.

How many excuses could I have made not to create this book and put myself out there? I have fears and uncertainty with this too, but I took action anyway.

Throughout this book, I will continue to stress the importance of making a decision to take responsibility and take action.

Please understand that nothing I share with you in this book will work if you don't take action with 100% commitment. There is no point going through this half-arsed.

How badly do you want to succeed?

Are you willing to push through your fears and seek help from other students?

Are you willing to make changes to your current lifestyle and make sacrifices?

These are some tough decisions you will have to make as you read through this book. Whether or not you take action could be the make or break for you in achieving first class marks.

Some university students are always looking for a magic bullet to solve their problems. "I can't manage time effectively." "I can't discipline myself enough to work efficiently, and I'm just bored."

"So, do you have a solution for this?"

Yes and No.

Yes, I can show you practical steps you can take based on my real life experiences and research. At the end of the day, this is meaningless if you don't make that personal decision and say to yourself 'enough is enough'. Take control of the areas in your life holding you back from achieving your dreams.

No more excuses! This was what I had to come to terms with when going into final year; it was now all on me. Now, it's all on YOU.

STEP 2

BEGIN WITH THE END IN MIND

"Where there is no vision the people perish."
- Proverbs 29:18

As our first step towards taking responsibility, we are going to be making use of this powerful yet often overlooked tool – your mind.

The power of a clear vision and clear goals cannot be underestimated in guiding you to make your dreams a reality. This is not some new age law of attraction nonsense; this is a timeless truth that has been in action since the beginning of time.

The clearer the vision in your mind and the stronger you can connect to the emotions of actually achieving it, the higher the probability that you will make it a reality.

Why? Because you will actually begin to believe it is possible.

The vision will drive you to take a completely different set of actions to make it a reality, and the more positive feedback you receive, the more you actually believe it can be done.

You know deep down inside what you really want. For many of you, one thing is at the root core of all your academic problems.

Is it a first class degree, but you're playing it down for a 2.1 degree, instead? You know what your dream degree is. What is holding you back from actually taking action?

LACK OF SELF-BELIEF

The truth is, subconsciously, you may not really believe it is possible, and you may have little self-confidence in your ability to make it happen.

I have designed this book to challenge all your assumptions and beliefs on what it takes to make it possible.

Hopefully, by the time you finish this book, your mind will be more open to the possibility and reality that your dream can become a reality.

This is why we must begin in your mind. Your thoughts affect your emotions, your actions, and the final results in your life. By becoming clear about your dreams and vision, you will have a solid foundation and direction for your future success.

Your mind is like a GPS navigation system. If you give it clear instructions about where it should go, it will do everything it can to keep you in check. If you step out of the route, it will let you know.

All of a sudden, you will feel uncomfortable wasting time, like browsing the internet instead of working on your assignment. How you "feel" will no longer determine whether or not you begin to prepare for your tutorials and exams early.

I strongly advise you: do not skip this step.

REAL LIFE:

//

I knew that I needed to have a first class average mark in final year to graduate with my desired degree. Now, I had to get very clear on this vision and put some real emotion into it.

As I lay down in my bed, I pulled out my phone, scrolled to a song from my gym playlist, and closed my eyes. Then, I started to daydream. Let's do this together:

You're seated in the graduation hall, in your suit and gown; no feeling can come close to describing this moment. You never thought you would make it to this position; you're still in a state of shock.

You turn around to look at the crowd. Your father and mother are happily seated together. Your father gives you a thumbs-up, and your mother is trying to keep her tears and emotions in control. They didn't believe you would make it, but you did, and they are proud of you.

You gaze in another direction of the hall. You see the students with whom you've come on the journey, the ones who helped you along the way, and then in the distance, you see the lecturers, tutors, and experts who doubted you and didn't believe you would make it. You hold no grudges; today is a day of celebration and victory.

The student standing ahead of you in the queue has just collected their degree from the graduation ceremony leader; there's loud clapping around the hall then the hall goes quiet...3...2...1.

The ceremony master, holding your degree, calls your name and says:

"Please step forward."

In that moment, all the hard work, all the perseverance, and all the ups and downs are worth it; the dream has now become real. You put a grin on your face, and in your mind, you say "I did it!" You collect your hard-earned degree and look around the hall.

You see all the doubters, the supporters, the haters, and altogether everyone acknowledges your success in a loud roar of clapping and standing ovation. Your dream has just become a reality.

OK STOP!

Let's not get too carried away with this process. Did you have the feeling of actually experiencing the scenario above? This is the key to effective "visualization".

It is this feeling that will make the vision seem more and more possible in your mind. It is this sort of clarity of your vision in mind, body, and soul that will drive you beyond your most difficult and frustrating periods of final year.

Every day, in my final year, I took time out to replay this vision. I would lie down on my bed, close my eyes, play some music, and visualize that I had already achieved my dreams. Whenever I struggled to find motivation and drive, I would step aside and rekindle these emotions from within. If it worked for me, it can work for you.

To help you recreate this for yourself and as part of your bonuses (which you will find at the end of the book), I have created a simple worksheet where you can write down your own vision and dream. After you're done, I would like you to stick this vision somewhere you can constantly remind yourself.

TAKEAWAY AND SUMMARY:

- Nobody cares about your excuses and why you didn't achieve the success you dreamed about; this is now all on you. Take full responsibility for your current and future situations, and take practical steps to make your dream a reality.

- Another crucial step towards your success is for you to begin with the end in mind. Create a clear vision in your mind and put some real emotion into it. Really see it, like it is real, and make sure to play out this vision as often as possible throughout the day. This vision will be your source of motivation, drive, and strength especially during periods you feel like giving up.

SECTION II

THE 4 HABITS OF HIGHLY SUCCESSFUL STUDENTS

Intro

"We are what we repeatedly do.
Excellence, then, is not an act, but a habit."
-Aristotle

If you've been following, you should now have a clear written vision and goal for your graduation degree. You've also made a decision to take full responsibility for where you are now and what your final results will be. Those two steps are crucial foundations for your future success.

If you remember, in Section I, I made an important statement:

> *"Your beliefs and mindset will determine your emotions, your actions, and eventually, your final results."*

We are going to further develop this in SECTION II. But for now, let's get practical. If you want top results, then you need to adopt the mindset, habits, and lifestyle of a highly successful student. These are the students who achieve the first class marks you desire.

What exactly is going on in their minds when they approach academic work? How do they balance the rest of their lifestyle? What sort of actions do they take that contribute to their strong final year results? How do I even know I am on the right track for success?

These are the kind of questions I will be answering, specifically, in SECTION II and throughout the book. All the information will be drawn directly from my personal experiences and my interactions with highly successful students.

Most importantly, I will structure all of this into simple steps and lessons that you can apply immediately, so that you can achieve similar results.

As I explain each of these habits and lessons, I recommend that you focus your attention on the ones that you aren't currently applying and decide which ones to implement.

Realistically, you will find that these habits and lessons are not a "one size fits all", and there will always be students who have done exceptionally well without applying some of the habits discussed here. The key is to test these strategies and find out what works for you, because you are unique!

I have already stressed the importance of your mindset in Section I. In addition to your mindset, there are 4 crucial lifestyle areas (Academics, Social, Spiritual, and Health) that are key to achieving the success you desire.

The habits are simply actions that continuously reinforce and hold all these lifestyle areas and your mindset together. That's how it all comes together.

Let's begin!

HABIT 1

SEEK FIRST TO UNDERSTAND AND THEN BE UNDERSTOOD

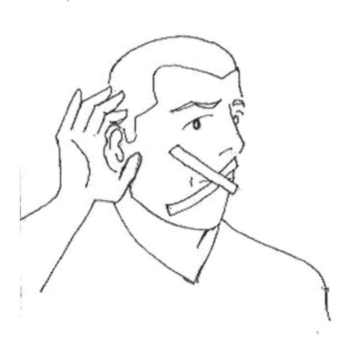

Why should you even bother putting in long hours, effort, and energy to "understand" your course content? Surely, it would be much easier to put your cramming abilities to use or avoid the topic completely to save time.

This is a logical conclusion, especially if you've been able to get away with this so far in your academic experiences. Are you willing to take that risk again in final year? I don't think so.

Understanding your course content becomes progressively important as you advance from a first year student to your final years at university.

I've spoken to enough examiners and lecturers to know that they are actively looking to separate the students, who show independent thinking and a strong understanding of the course content, from those who don't. It's point blank, staring at you in your course syllabus mark scheme! Seriously, have a look at the assessment criteria for the top band of marks given; you'll see why this is crucial for your success.

Consciously or unconsciously, highly successful students have made a personal decision to make understanding – and not memorizing their academic work – a priority.

They will typically go through strenuous lengths to simply understand a concept that other students believe to be irrelevant or unnecessary. They will pursue lecturers or other students, read journals, etc., just to make sense of concepts they do not understand.

Several times in my final year, I would follow some very "keen" students, who would attend non-course related lectures, usually offered to the public. These lectures would only touch on a few concepts in our actual core material of the course, but they would cover a lot of wider information, usually current state of affairs, statistics, and other information, which would greatly improve my understanding of the actual course content.

Initially, these offshoot seminars and lectures appeared to be a waste of time, but when time came for examinable work to be handed in, I was easily able to use this extra information and my deeper understanding to achieve much higher marked work.

By seeking to truly understand, you are essentially storing this information in your long-term memory and in a much more personal, independent way.

On the flip side, when you extensively practise "cramming" and rote memorization, you significantly reduce the amount of information that is retained as well as the duration of the retention.

This clear advantage of understanding over cramming was demonstrated in a real, simulated undergraduate classroom by Kapler, Weston and Wiseheart (2015).

In this simulated study, 169 undergraduates were presented with scientific curriculum. Some were told to cram the material over a one-day span, but others were told to review the information daily. At the end of the review period, the final tests and examinations results showed that the students who practised a cramming method of studying had overall worse grades than the rest of the students.

When you eventually have to recall this information in exams or written work, you will find that you go into "freestyle" mode. This is when you begin to express your deep understanding in an independent, coherent, original, and creative way.

If the examiners are women or men you are trying to win over, then this is how you would do it. This is what gets them excited about marking your work and giving you more marks!

That subtle, mental decision to put in that extra effort to understand topics you don't understand will make or break your final year results.

Even though the initial energy and time spent on understanding a concept outweighs memorizing it, in the long run it is ten times more rewarding than memorizing!

The students who have spent most of their energies on memorization will have to revisit the concept over and over again, because it will continue to remain in their short-term memory.

What if the examiner twists the wordings of the exam questions in a way that you didn't prepare for? You'd get absolutely screwed over, because you only memorized the information in a one-dimensional, specific context.

Okay, so hopefully now you understand why "understanding" is so important. So how can you develop this deep level of understanding in your university course?

The first strategy in achieving this deep understanding is "Active Recall".

This is a simple mental exercise where you practise recalling or retrieving the information you have learnt from memory the best you can. It's similar to running until exhaustion. This is clearly the opposite of passive learning, such as reading.

To test this out, J.D. Karpicke and H.L. Roediger, III (2008) conducted a study on college students. They instructed a select group of college students to study 40 pairs of foreign language words on flash cards and came to the conclusion that active recall was integral for learning.

TRY THIS QUICK EXERCISE NOW

Get a blank piece of paper, and in the middle, write down the name of a movie or music album you love.

Without checking the Internet for answers, I want you to brainstorm as many characters from that movie or all the songs from the album you can remember. You could go even deeper, detailing the exact role that character played in the movie, the movie plot, etc. You get the point though; you can go really deep here.

How did you do? Did you struggle? Most likely, you put in a good amount of mental focus, strain, and effort to map things out. You probably failed in your attempts to address some tricky concepts and ideas. Perfect!

All that matters is what we do with these gaps of knowledge. The more we can close these gaps, the greater our understanding and the better our final results will be.

This is why practice tests, tutorial work, and all those annoying lecture quizzes are so valuable. The feedback from this "non-examined work" will help deepen your understanding.

LESSON #1: FAILURE IS ONLY FEEDBACK: FAIL HARD PRIVATELY, SO YOU CAN HAVE MEGA SUCCESS PUBLICLY

> *"I've missed more than 9000 shots in my career. I've lost almost 300 games. 26 times, I've been trusted to take the game winning shot and missed. I've failed over and over and over again in my life. And that is why I succeed."* - **Michael Jordan**

Oftentimes, we limit ourselves to a few sources when learning something new or challenging. Typically, in university, these limited sources will be lecture and textbook material. To truly understand your university course, you have to move beyond the one-dimensional and one-sided opinions in the lecture notes and even the course textbooks! You have to embrace:

LESSON #2: Y.O.L.O.

YOU

ONLY

LEARN

OUTSIDE

No, this isn't the "You. Only. Live. Once." mindset. I'm definitely not recommending you abandon your graduation dreams and go crazy, living for the moment, in final year.

What I mean is this:

You. Only. Learn. Outside.

Outside where? Outside the four walls of your course lectures, textbooks, and materials.

Don't get me wrong. Attending lectures and having a strong foundational understanding of your course-provided textbooks are a crucial first step, but they are heavily limiting your potential.

My reason for YOLO is simple: YOU ARE UNIQUE.

The course textbooks and lectures are simply one person's perspective on the course or topic. Most likely, you can't relate to the way they explain ideas or solutions. It doesn't mean you can't learn and understand that particular topic; it just means you have to search 'outside' this material and find sources that speak your language.

Here's an example:

Let's say, we're trying to understand how increased employment in a country can contribute to a greater standard of living for the average citizen. You've already been to lectures and read the textbook chapters, but you're still missing a deeper understanding. Right off the top of my head, I can already think of other sources 'outside' that will help you with this:

- Internet articles and websites
- Relevant magazines, like "The Economist"
- YouTube tutorials or general news on economy videos
- Relevant audio podcasts
- Online academic journals for a more professional and sophisticated view on the issue
- Speaking to fellow course mates
- Attending office hours and speaking to lecturers
- Seminars, workshops, and non-course related lectures
- Participating in online debates or forums

I could go on and on and on. The key point is that real learning happens outside what has been given to you by your lecturers. By seeking to learn from a wide range of different sources, you will engage your entire mind and body senses to understand that topic. This is how you can achieve deep understanding and mastery of any area of your course content.

Curiosity, to deepen your understanding and close your gaps of knowledge, will lead you to the right sources. 9 times out of 10, a student that is interested in their course or particular topic will be naturally curious to learn more.

Unfortunately, I suspect many of you aren't particularly passionate about your course or units within it. No problem, I was in the same situation going into final year. Here's what I discovered:

LESSON #3: PURSUE EFFORT AND THE PASSION WILL FOLLOW

It's really simple. The more work you put into something, the more you seek to understand and conquer it, and the more passion you will have for it. Curiosity will naturally follow, and the rest is history.

If you've ever put in some real effort to date someone who was "playing hard to get", you most likely found yourself caught up in the "thrill of the chase".

I became very passionate about closing the gaps in my knowledge. I searched YouTube videos, magazines, journals, and really anything that I could get a hold of to help me better understand what I was learning.

It became an exciting challenge to figure out the solution to a problem and understand a tough concept.

LESSON #4: IT'S NOT ABOUT YOU, SO GIVE THE EXAMINERS EXACTLY WHAT THEY WANT

I've already shown you that the #1 thing examiners look for is deep, independent, and original understanding. We've covered how to develop this in lessons #1 to #3.

This final lesson is a recap and icing on the cake for this habit. Seek to understand the examiner. These are typically your course lecturers and tutors.

Usually, with exam questions, tests, etc., too many students focus on giving the examiner what they think they want, or they focus entirely on answering their own created questions. When they fail the exam, they look around in confusion as if their results were rigged.

You can work super hard, but if you don't deliver your work in a way the examiners want, they will never give you the marks you desire.

If you can get into their minds and put yourself in their shoes, you have put yourself in a very powerful position. We've already taken the first crucial step to achieving this by seeking a deep understanding of the course content.

Here are other specific ideas on how you can get into the mind of the examiner:

- Use and learn the resources lecturers and tutors have given you already. You have a mark scheme for the syllabus, so read it carefully, and take note of what it requires to get the marks you want.

- Remember what I said about the importance of feedback. For every piece of work your lecturer and examiner marks, take the feedback as an indication of the style, method, and type of answers to questions that they like. Don't throw away or ignore marked work because you can't be bothered to review it!

- Cultivate an ongoing relationship with them. I will touch on this later in the book.

- Just ask them! When it all comes down to it, you could always, straight up, ask them what they are looking for exactly.

Once you're in a powerful position, where you truly "understand" your course content and your examiner, then you have full permission "to be understood". This is where you can begin to add your own personality, creativity, and display flair.

Essentially, this is the part of the habit where you hand in work that will be examined. As the examiner marks your work, they will be astonished. You are speaking their language, and they love it!

It's no surprise that students who pull this off well will typically score very strong marks. You will soon be this student.

HABIT 1 RECAP:

- A solid understanding of your course material is crucial for your success. Examiners will give you higher marks if you show them you have a deep understanding with independent thinking.

- Practise "active recall" and continue to hunt for feedback from as many sources as possible. This will help you close gaps in your knowledge and deepen your understanding.

- Embrace "You. Only. Learn. Outside. (YOLO)". Look outside your lecture notes and textbooks and allow yourself to explore the real world to further expand your understanding of the course material.

- Make a decision to actively seek knowledge, put in the work, and you will find that the passion and curiosity to learn more will naturally increase.

- Give examiners exactly what they want; use the feedback they have given you to gauge this, or directly ask them what they expect. Once you understand what they want, you can deliver this in examined work and "be understood".

LESSONS:

- **Lesson #1:**   Failure is only feedback: fail hard privately so you can have mega success publicly.

- **Lesson #2:**   Y.O.L.O. (You. Only. Learn. Outside.)

- **Lesson #3:**   Pursue effort, and the passion will follow.

- **Lesson #4:**   It's not about you, so give the examiners exactly what they want.

HABIT 2

SURROUND YOURSELF WITH PEOPLE THAT SUPPORT YOUR DREAM

Real Life:

I saw her from across the lecture hall; I had never really spoken to her since I had come into University, but this wasn't the time to be shy or proud. So after the lecture, I walked up to her and said, "Hey, we haven't really spoken before, but I just thought I'd come over and talk to you."

She turned around and smiled, "Oh, okay what's going on?" Then I replied, "Erm…Well, I kinda screwed up last year's results, and now I need first class marks to graduate with good honours. I don't quite know where to start or even what to do. I was going to ask if, from time to time, I could ask you to explain certain topics to me and *cough* maybe if you need any help I could help you out as well?"

Long Pause.

I didn't know what answer to expect. As far as I could tell, she was one of the most academically gifted students in my course, and I had just stepped outside my comfort zone to seek her help.

I couldn't really get pissed if she rejected my offer. After all, I hadn't spoken to her in this manner from first year up until now. I just thought she was way too "keen" to be my friend at the time. I thought I had appeared like a desperate leech looking for help.

She giggled, "Yeah, sure! I would love to. When should we start? Maybe I should bring a marker pen so we can use the whiteboard in an empty classroom, and I can coach you."

What?! She actually wants to help me. Even to teach me. For freeeeee?!!! I stepped out in faith, and it looked like I got rewarded beyond my expectations.

It was easy for me to avoid talking to her. I could have been arrogant or prideful and said, "Hey, I don't need anyone's help. I will achieve success on my own."

I learnt a valuable lesson:

You cannot achieve your dreams on your own.
You have to develop relationships with likeminded people who will support, encourage, and guide you towards this dream.

From that point forward, I had established the most valuable relationship, which set me up for success in my final year results. She put in time, effort, and energy to explain tough concepts and problems to me every time I was stuck, and she did so with enthusiasm. She coached me on the mindset of a highly successful student and brought me up to her level of thinking.

Why would she do this? What was in this for her?

Remember what I mentioned in habit 1: Highly successful students seek to understand first, then be understood.

By teaching a struggling student, she was effectively putting herself in a position to further deepen her understanding of the course material. Whenever I asked her tough questions she didn't know, she would go and seek help outside the lecture halls to close that gap in knowledge and understanding.

Can you see how the cycle works? By genuinely looking to help other students, you can further deepen your understanding.

I noticed something about her social circle and the students from whom she often sought help:

LESSON #5: SURROUND YOURSELF WITH LIKEMINDED, SUCCESS-DRIVEN STUDENTS

Keep hanging around the same type of people, and you will continue to get the same results. If you are not getting the academic results you desire and/or wish to maximize the chances of getting the degree you want, you must closely examine the type of students with whom you spend the majority of your time.

The type of students you hang around will significantly affect your mindset, thoughts, and approach to your academic work. Eventually, it will show up in your results.

This is not the time to play around.

In a study done by the US National Science Foundation, it was found that students who were in a social network of students with higher grades than their own were more likely to improve their grades.

I am not telling you to cut off relationships with your closest friends or to leech onto successful students. What I am saying is, by surrounding yourself with success-driven and likeminded students, you can exponentially increase your chances of success.

In my case, I found myself in an entirely new social circle. I was surrounded by students who were hungry for success.

Whenever I would say something wasn't possible, they would ask, "Why not?" Whenever I wanted to settle for average results, they would rebuke me. Whenever I wanted to skimp in my work, they would make me feel guilty. They showed me more effective ways to work, how to form relationships with lecturers, etc.

Can you see how this further developed my self-belief and confidence that I could accomplish my dream?

By surrounding yourself with and emulating successful students, you will eventually adopt their self-belief and habits of success. And then, guess what?

You become successful.

This is a no brainer. Learn from and adopt success, and you will become successful.

Your social life doesn't stop with students. We can go further, much further than even graduates. We can go straight to the source of all the information you need to succeed.

LESSON #6: DEVELOP A WORKING RELATIONSHIP WITH TUTORS AND LECTURERS

Remember, in Habit 1: Lesson #4, I highlighted that it was crucial to truly understand what the examiners are looking for. These examiners are typically your lecturers and tutors.

In most cases, they have chosen this profession because they are passionate about a particular section of the university course. Even though it may not seem like it, they are also human beings – just like you – with fears, aspirations, and dreams for their future.

Get to know them on a personal level. I'm sure you will have something in common with them beyond academics. Become a familiar face by showing up for office hours and after lectures. Stick around to speak to them or even help them out, if need be.

Why should you care about doing this?

These are the people who are going to mark your work and decide on your final graduation degree!

How will you understand them and what they want if you don't have a mutual working relationship with them?

Why would a tutor help you understand concepts for an exam when you only show up for office hours, in the last few days before an exam, towards the end of the year?!

Why would a tutor or lecturer give you an indication of where you should focus your study and exactly how they want your answers if they don't know you personally?

By developing a working relationship with your tutors and lecturers, you will have further access to valuable information and knowledge that other students wouldn't have.

You will also have access to the insight of an "expert" in the field, and this will help you understand your course material better.

HABIT 2 RECAP:

- Final year is not the time to be proud and arrogant. Humble yourself and ask for help if you need it.

- Socialize and surround yourself with likeminded, success-driven students, and over time, you will find that their "can do" attitude will rub off on you.

- Understanding what the examiner is looking for is crucial for your success. So take the time to develop a personal and working relationship with them.

LESSONS:
- **Lesson #5:**   Surround yourself with likeminded, success-driven students.
- **Lesson #6:**   Develop a working relationship with tutors and lecturers.

HABIT 3

Take Care of Your Mind, Body and Spirit

Real life:

//

I had written down exactly what I wanted to achieve. I was very clear in my mind that I was willing to take action, but I still felt like something was missing. I had grown up in a Christian home, but I had walked away from my commitment to God a long time ago.

Now that I found myself in an impossible situation that required the miraculous to achieve my dreams, I completely humbled myself to God for help, and I recommitted myself to my faith. From that moment onward, I felt a great sense of peace and guidance beyond my own understanding and comprehension. I immediately dedicated myself to consistent, daily prayer and a Bible reading routine.

Next up was my body and health. I booked myself for a couple of sessions with a health coach and immediately drew up a healthy diet plan of what I would and wouldn't allow myself to eat and drink. I followed this with a sustainable workout plan that included weight training, football, sprinting, and basketball.

"

I predict that many who read this will find that it appears counter-intuitive. Why should you waste time working out, exercising, meditating, and praying? How on earth will this contribute to your final year results?

Throughout this book, I will stress the importance of your mind and why I believe it is truly the key to your success.

While I do not wish to impose my beliefs on anyone, I would be a complete liar to ignore the fact that developing my spiritual life contributed significantly to my final results. Balancing one's spiritual life means different things for different people. Some people focus on quiet meditation, and others focus on prayer. Find whatever works for you.

LESSON #7: A WELL-BALANCED SPIRITUAL LIFE CONTRIBUTES
SIGNIFICANTLY TO YOUR PEACE OF MIND

In my personal experience, I found that prayer, going to church weekly, and reading encouraging scriptures in the Bible gave me a deep sense of peace, to the point that, I completely stopped worrying about my final year results. Think about the decisions we make that damage our progress, because we struggle to trust the process.

I have witnessed students push themselves way too hard because they don't feel like they have "worked hard enough". This eventually leads to burnout, and negatively affects their results. Worry, anxiety, fear, burnout, and stress are usually a direct result of lack of trust in the process.

When I let go of control of the outcome to a "higher power", I was able to relax, stay calm, and trust the process completely. I was able to discipline myself to stay on top of my academic assignments without overworking myself. I managed my time better, absorbed information much quicker, and enjoyed the journey.

Honestly, I have no scientific evidence to back this up. When I completely let go of control over my final year results, it seemed as if everything I needed to achieve my dreams fell into place perfectly. I met the right people, who gave me the right support at the right time. I happened to stumble across resources to study for the right topics that showed up in the exams, and so on.

Peace of mind, trusting the process, and guidance from a "higher power" – these are the main benefits you will get from developing this area.

Okay, but why should you worry about your body and health?

Lesson #8: Your body (health) is the main source of your energy

I won't waste your time talking about the many studies available and benefits of a good, healthy lifestyle because you already know this. The importance of good sleeping habits, a healthy diet, and an exercise routine is common knowledge.

The key point is that poor health can negatively impact your final year results.

Here's an example. Remember those late weekday nights out, where you let loose, drank, and ate a lot of unhealthy stuff. You knew you had lectures the next day at 9 am, but hey, who cares?!

You stumble back to bed around 3 am and crash. A few hours later, your alarm wakes you up. It's time for lectures.

Do you remember how you felt? Did you feel like "death" itself had come upon you?

Most likely, you shut the alarm off, went back to sleep, and missed your lectures. If you managed to drag yourself to lectures, you probably completely zoned out, with your eyes half open. It's a deadly combo: lack of sleep and an unhealthy diet.

In my experience, two things stand out when we don't take care of our body:

- The energy, motivation, drive, and discipline to take action on our goals significantly reduce.

- We waste more energy to accomplish the same tasks, so we become much more unproductive.

In a report of studies on the consequences of sleep deprivation amongst college students, Hershner and Chervin (2014) showed how lack of sleep negatively affects learning, memory retention, emotions, and potentially, the final grades of the students.

Your body may begin to shut down towards the end of the year, because you had been putting it under an immense amount of stress throughout the year.

Unfortunately, at that point, there's no going back, and nobody will care that your poor health was the reason you ended up with poor results.

Take care of your body, and it will give you the necessary energy you need to get through final year productively.

HABIT 3 RECAP:

- A healthy balance of the body and the soul positively reinforces your mind, which is the key for your success.

- A well-balanced spiritual life will give you the necessary peace of mind to keep you on the path to your dreams.

- Take good care of your body; this will give you the necessary energy you need for the long, tedious journey in final year.

LESSONS:

- **Lesson #7:**   A well-balanced spiritual life contributes significantly to your peace of mind.

- **Lesson #8:**   Your body (health) is the main source of your energy.

HABIT 4

Don't Manage Time; "Own" It

Real life:

❞
     I was right in the middle of final year and constantly under pressure to stay on top of my work. That wasn't all. I was also captain of a football team, the events manager of a charity group, a volunteer for a disabled and elderly charity society, and a participant in other extracurricular activities. This was on top of my commitment to maintain a steady social, spiritual, and healthy lifestyle.

Time became my most valuable asset in final year. Every minute I wasted having "small talk" with people, playing video games, surfing the Internet, and messing around made me extremely uncomfortable.

At the back of my mind, I knew I should be doing something much more productive. I tried to "manage" my time, detailing my to-do lists and fit all my plans inside. This did very little to help me. So, I made a decision to no longer be at the mercy of my to-do list. I decided to completely dominate and own my time, instead.

II

Out of all the habits discussed so far, one idea clearly stands out:

LESSON #9: SPEND THE MAJORITY OF YOUR TIME ON PROFITABLE ACTIVITIES

In habit 1, we saw that by focusing our time and energy to "seek first to understand, and then be understood", we are in a much better position to achieve higher marks from the examiners.

In habit 2, we saw that spending more time developing relationships with likeminded students, lecturers and tutors will directly benefit your work ethic, beliefs, understanding of the examiners, and eventually, your final year results.

In habit 3, we looked at the link between the mind, body, and spirit. Time spent keeping a healthy balance of our "spirit" and "body" will give us the necessary peace of mind and vital energy needed to complete the year successfully.

If university were a business competition, time would represent the amount of money you have to accomplish your financial goals.

The money is limited; so if you waste the money making bad investment decisions, you can't get that money back, and you make a loss.

If instead, you make profitable investment decisions, you get your money back and make additional profits. That is why time is the most valuable asset you have available to you in final year.

Now in habit 4, I'd like us to go deeper into the idea of time management, because I have a problem with mainstream time "management" and overcomplicated to-do lists.

Typically, these methods of organizing your time and planning give little room for:

- Unexpected events, such as emergency activities that pop up
- Prioritization of activities and plans
- Variation in the quality of activities and plans

Managing time suggests that we are at the mercy of our to-do lists; why not "own" it instead?

This means, we will separate our tasks into what is and isn't important, and then choose freely to focus the majority of our time and effort on the important tasks. By "owning" time, instead, you dominate your to-do lists and not the other way around. You have more freedom to plan for the unexpected, prioritize activities, and allow for variations in them.

Following my business analogy, imagine you have been given a certain amount of money to be invested profitably. After doing your research, you discover that there are some business opportunities with the potential for much more profit than others and some clearly standing out as a "catch".

You, then, decide to invest a larger portion of your money into the opportunities that stood out, less money for next best, and so on.

To allow for flexibility and unexpected events, such as the cost of investment rising, you make sure to keep some money in your savings account, just in case things don't go as planned.

If I take the analogy and replace money with time, and I replace business opportunities with your to-do list, can you understand why "owning" time is much better than "managing" it?

To-do lists aren't completely useless; we can still take the usual list and "own" time, instead.

Let's say your lists of plans for today are the following:

- Write out plan for dissertation
- Go for a run
- Buy food and cook
- Complete tutorial assignment for tomorrow
- Go for office hours at 4 pm for follow-up questions
- Call friends: Richard, Michael, and Mitchell
- Attend lectures at 10 am - 1 pm
- Society team meeting at 2.30 pm
- Call family: mum, dad, and bro
- Call girlfriend
- Morning prayers

Okay, so let's take this to-do list and "own" it. Reorder the list, assigning:

Urgent activities (U): These are the most important activities that need to be addressed as soon as possible.

Important activities (I): These are also important activities but do not have to be addressed immediately and are not as important as the urgent activities.

Uncategorized (no symbol is assigned for this): These are activities that would fall at the bottom of the list in terms of priority and urgency. So typically, these events may be urgent but definitely not important, for example, a friend telling you to call them back as soon as possible because they have some gossip for you.

Here we go:

- Morning prayers (U)
- Attend lectures at 10 am - 1 pm (U)
- Society team meeting at 2.30 pm (U)
- Complete tutorial assignment for tomorrow (U)
- Write out plan for dissertation (I)
- Go for a run (I)
- Buy food and cook (I)
- Go for office hours at 4 pm for follow-up questions (I)
- Call family: mum, dad, and bro (I)
- Meet up with girlfriend (I)
- Call friends: Richard, Michael, and Mitchell

Okay, we're almost done, but we can take this further, reordering by rank in order of most profitable "business opportunities."

1. Morning prayers (U)
2. Attend lectures at 10 am - 1 pm (U)
3. Complete tutorial assignment for tomorrow (U)
4. Society team meeting at 2.30 pm (U)
5. Go for office hours at 4 pm for follow-up questions (I)
6. Go for a run (I)
7. Buy food and cook (I)
8. Meet with girlfriend (I)
9. Write out plan for dissertation (I)
10. Call family: mum, dad, and bro (I)
11. Call friends: Richard, Michael, and Mitchell

We're done!

So now, we have our activities and plans prioritized and ranked in order of importance, urgency, and quality. Right off the bat, I know the first two urgent activities need to be crossed off my list before the day ends. I won't be wasting too much time on one activity since I know there are more I need to take care of before the end of the day.

Once all urgent activities are completed, I have much more flexibility with the important ones. This way, should something unexpected pop up; I'd be able to sacrifice some important activities to cover, instead of the urgent activities, and likewise for unimportant activities.

This method of prioritizing and distributing your time is not a one-size fit for all. You may be managing a job on the side or even have kids in addition to what is already on your list.

The key point is:

LESSON #10: TIME IS THE MOST VALUABLE RESOURCE YOU HAVE, SO INVEST IT WISELY

****A quick note on procrastination****

By "owning" time and properly prioritizing activities, you can significantly decrease your amount of procrastination simply because you have a clearer plan of action for what activities to cross off the list as soon as possible.

Most likely, you would feel some level of discomfort if you have an unfinished activity marked as "urgent", but you are wasting time looking at pictures on Instagram. This discomfort, combined with your balance in the other areas of your lifestyle, will give you the necessary discipline to reduce procrastination. In 'the extras' section of Part 2 of this book I will show you in more in-depth detail how to overcome procrastination, eliminate distractions and deal with lack of motivation.

HABIT 4 RECAP:

- Forget time "management" of your to-do list; "own" and dominate it instead.

- Owning your time will give you more flexibility to prioritize, rank, and change your daily activities.

- Time is limited; it is also the most valuable resource you have available to you, so spend it wisely.

- By having a clear plan of action for your activities before the day begins, you can eliminate a lot of procrastination because you will feel a greater urge to cross the activities off your list.

LESSONS:

- **Lesson #9:**   Spend the majority of your time on profitable activities.

- **Lesson #10:**   Time is the most valuable resource you have, so invest it wisely.

SECTION III

THE END IS NEAR:
THE REAL FINAL PUSH

"If you are going through hell, keep going."

-Winston Churchill

Introduction

Final year of university has many similarities with a long distance race. You've all been forced, at some point, to participate in this when you were younger.

You had several strategies for the race.

Option 1:   You could sprint from the start. But then, towards the end of the race, you probably found your legs got really tired, and you ended up falling behind, finishing the race with poor timing. In final year, this is the student who overworks himself or herself too early and burns out towards the end of the year.

Option 2:   On the other extreme, you could start the race by putting in little effort, jogging at a very comfortable pace without pushing yourself, and then towards the end of the race, sprint hard to catch up, finishing the race with poor timing as well. In final year, these are the students who don't push themselves to work diligently early on, and then as deadlines approach, they frantically attempt to regain all the lost ground.

The perfect balance is in the middle. Start the race with a consistent steady pace where you're pushing yourself, but not so hard that you run out of energy. As the finish line approaches, you have enough energy to run faster and sprint past the finish line comfortably in good time.

In Sections I and II, I addressed how you could start the race well and maintain this perfect balance. We spoke about, first, getting clear on your vision, getting rid of excuses, and then plotting out a plan of action. You've learned and, hopefully, been applying the essential habits in Section II that will help you maintain a steady consistent work ethic, positively reinforce your mindset, and bring you a lot closer to achieving your graduation dreams.

Now in Section III, I will talk about the last leg of the race. This is the last sprint to the finish line: this is the real final push.

This is the period when important deadlines and crucial examinations are approaching fast. Revision comes into the picture, and students begin to chase lecturers for last minute advice. Typically, at this point, the nerves begin to kick in, and fear creeps in.

Non-clinical anxiety, stress, depression, burnout, panic, and fear are not uncommon problems at this point. If left uncontrolled, these problems can negatively and significantly affect your final results. All your hard work will be undone.

I heard of a university student who walked into final year with a first class mark average and ended up graduating with a 3rd class overall degree, because he panicked under exam pressure and failed crucial exams.

Fortunately, with the help I have given you in this book, this will not happen to you.

2 RADICAL AND EFFECTIVE SOLUTIONS FOR (P.A.D.S)

Panic

Anxiety

Depression

Stress

Panic, Anxiety, Depression, and Stress (PADS) are the top four common emotional problems with which university students struggle, especially as exams approach. I would add burnout, but typically, it is a by-product of these four.

There is a ton of free information online about how to overcome these issues, some of which are valuable information. The rest, quite honestly, is nonsense.

Regurgitating common information will not be of value to you, so I've narrowed down 2 uncommon, radical, and effective solutions to PADS.

Disclaimer: These solutions only address non-clinical PADS. If you decide to take action on any of these solutions, do so at your own risk, and please consult your GP/Doctor if you currently have or have a history of health problems related to these solutions.

You ready?

Reader discretion is advised!

RADICAL SOLUTION #1: MINIMIZE OR ELIMINATE BAD SUGARS FROM YOUR DIET

"Good" (Natural) sugars are found in "whole foods", which are foods that have not been altered from their natural state. These kinds of food include typical fresh veggies and fruits and are bundled with vitamins, minerals, and all that healthy good stuff.

"Bad" (Unnatural) sugars are typically found in processed foods that have been altered from their natural state. Typically, in the ingredients labels, there are added sugars usually ending in "– ose" (sucrose, fructose, etc.), corn syrup, and so on.

Once again, the importance of cutting sugar from our diet is already common knowledge, and the media is constantly pounding on and on about this. I won't waste time repeating common knowledge. I want to focus on the way excessive, unnatural sugar intake can affect PADS and, eventually, your final year exam results.

Here's another simple analogy:

Do you remember the last time you had a ridiculous crush on someone?

Every time you saw and spoke to the person, you would get these uncontrollable weird butterflies inside.

Whenever they gave you attention, you were beaming on cloud 9; you were happy. As soon as they wouldn't reply to your text messages or return your phone calls, and they began to ignore you, it felt like someone had punched you in the gut, and you hit a low.

Then, all of a sudden, they send you a message again, and then you're excited. Just like a yo-yo, your emotions keep going up and down, never really at a stable point. When you're on the high, you're happy, excited and full of energy. When you hit the low, you're mellow, anxious, and experience PADS.

In my analogy, bad sugar represents the person you have a crush on. That same effect of highs and lows they put you through is exactly the same as what sugar does to your body.

When you first take the sugar, you have a spike in "good" feelings. A few hours later, you crash and feel horrible and then the cycle repeats over and over again. This is why sugar contributes to PADS. Your hormones are not operating at the natural stable level, because you keep altering them by consuming sugar.

Research on heavy consumers of bad sugars has shown that the massive rollercoaster swings in blood sugar levels worsen mood disorder symptoms and anxiety and negatively affect learning and memory.

Let's say you decide to stop obsessing over this person you have a crush on. After a couple of weeks, you no longer really care if they send you a message or not. In fact, you're so busy with other things you don't even notice.

Your emotions become more stable, and instead of being worried and anxious about them replying to you, you're calm, relaxed, and chilled out. This is what happens when bad sugar begins to clear out from your body.

There's too much fluff and over-complication on healthy eating and nutrition. After studying and experimenting with my nutrition for over 10 years, I've simplified everything into one statement:

"If the food you are about to eat did not exist in a similar form 100 years ago and you do not understand some of the jargon on the ingredients label, then you're much safer not eating it."

RADICAL SOLUTION #2: TAKE REGULAR EXTENDED FASTING INTERVALS

For the purposes of this book, a fast is defined as "an extended period of time where you eat nothing."
Simple.

We all fast, especially when we are asleep. In this case, I'm talking about extending the period of time between meals when you are still awake.

There are different variations of this:

Full 24 hours without eating with a meal to break the fast in-between.

Regularly eating during a specific time period, like only eating from 12 pm - 6 pm every day.

One day of eating normally followed by a 24-hour fast the next day. Repeat the cycle.

3 days back-to-back fasting only once every month.

It really comes down to you and your lifestyle. If you have sports commitments or an intensive workout on a particular day, it's probably best you break your fast before this, so you have energy. Personally, I was able to still play sports and work out in a fasted state.

In the fitness world, this type of fasting where you consciously choose not to eat at certain mealtimes is called "intermittent fasting".

I first came across this during my consultation with a nutritionist. Immediately, I adopted this into my lifestyle. From 11 am to 6 pm, I would freely eat, but

after this period, I ate nothing and only drank water.
The experiment paid off big-time:

1. My concentration and energy levels, especially in the morning, went through the roof. I had no problem waking up early for lectures, paying attention, and taking notes. This particularly paid off during exams; I was super alert and focused during all my papers.
2. Because I wasted less mental and physical energy thinking about, preparing, and eating food, my mind was much clearer, and I had more free time to accomplish my daily tasks. In other words, I became much more productive.
3. I became much more disciplined. Self-motivation became a non-issue because the discipline from restricting myself from eating translated to other areas of my life, especially my academic work and planning for deadlines.
4. I experienced a deep spiritual component with this. All my "brain fog" began to clear away, and most of my emotional problems reduced significantly.

BONUS: I got into the best shape I had ever been in my life: clear skin, solid fitness level, and low body fat percentage *sigh* (good old days). This is probably due to the increase of human growth hormone released from fasting.

A recent study (Fond et al., 2013) on the relationship between fasting and mood found that fasting participants experienced increased energy levels, decreased anxiety, and a general positive improvement in mood levels.

I'm not alone in this; there are tons of testimonials online. The key point is to experiment and see what works for you. Maybe you decide to take a 3-day fast once every month, no problem. Find whatever works for you and stick to it. Over time, you will find that your experience of PADS will drastically reduce.

Side note on withdrawal symptoms*

Although the two solutions I have suggested can be applied immediately, expect some initial withdrawal symptoms.

These include:

- Temporary anxiety
- Tiredness
- Sugar cravings
- Moodiness and irritability

It's almost like getting over an ex or someone you really like. It takes time. Relax and let your body readjust to a stable, normal state.

I also understand that it takes a relatively high level of discipline to implement these completely. If you don't have that discipline now, it's okay. Just start small and build up over time.

PADS RECAP:

- Panic, Anxiety, Depression, and Stress are the top four emotional problems you may face. These can easily hold you back from achieving your desired goals, but there are simple strategies to minimize or overcome them.

- One solution to PADS is to minimize or eliminate bad sugars from your diet. Excessive intake of bad sugars will cause massive yo-yo swings in your hormonal levels and eventually your emotions. By reducing your intake of bad sugars, you rebalance your emotions and regain your clarity of mind. I have one very simple piece of advice to help you decide what food to eat: "If the food you are about to eat did not exist in a similar form 100 years ago and you do not understand some of the jargon on the ingredients label, then you're much safer not eating it."

- Another solution to PADS is fasting. Whether you decide to fast daily, bi-weekly, or monthly, fasting is a great way to detox your body, rebalance your emotions, and improve your energy and concentration levels.

REVISION, EXAMS, AND ALL OTHER LAST MINUTE NONSENSE

The end of final year was literally around the corner, and I had already begun to feel the real gravity of the situation.

If there were any doubt about the importance of final year, other students around me made sure I knew. I saw final year students in a state of fear and panic. Some were in tears from

HEY BRO I CRAMMED SO HARD LAST NIGHT!

revision stress, and some just literally gave up all hope.

The library was as packed as a nightclub, and Red Bull drinks were the new alcohol.

Students would literally queue to get into the library from 6 am in the morning and wouldn't leave till midnight or even later! Some students even tried to sleep overnight to reserve their library desk space.

It wasn't uncommon, at this point, for a student to come up to me and ask me to explain course concepts that had been covered in the first weeks of final year, and then I think to myself:

"WHAT HAVE YOU BEEN DOING ALL YEAR?!"

Everything becomes a mind game. Some students almost scared me to death, telling me that certain exam topics may or may not show up in the exam or some solutions for past paper questions were wrong.

In the meantime, lecturers and tutors weren't particularly helpful. All of a sudden, they wouldn't assist as much during office hours, and when asked what to revise for exams, they were very vague in their answers.

LESSON #1: DON'T LET THE LAST MINUTE PANIC AND NONSENSE THROW YOU OFF YOUR GAME

At this point, I had done most of the hard work during the year; I refused to allow all this nonsense to distract me from my final goal.

Towards the end of any race, there will always be that last minute adrenaline and tension. There will always be a cheering crowd of people and a lot of noise around the finish line. I knew I had to stay focused.

By the time the final term had begun, I had already reviewed all my course modules and taken notes on the topics that I didn't understand. My mission, at this point, was to further close my gaps in knowledge and push for mastery of my course content.

I devised a clear strategy and spent a lot of time working on my exam technique, using past papers to prepare for the style of questions and structure of the exams.

I recreated real time exam conditions over and over again, with a real timer and practice paper questions.

For every question I got wrong or didn't understand, I would hunt down any source I could find for clarification.

The rest of my lifestyle was still intact. I was still working out, eating healthy, praying every morning, etc. This helped me maintain my focus, peace of mind, and productivity throughout this intense period.

Exams:

Exam day finally came round. My usual routine didn't change: sleep early, wake up early, pray, review work, shower, eat, and off to the exam hall at 9 am.

Often, I saw students outside exam halls, trying to discuss and solve last minute revision questions. I quickly avoided them; this was not a time for me to be distracted by learning or relearning anything. Even as I sat down in the exam hall before the exam began, I wouldn't allow myself to be distracted by the looks of fear and distress on other students' faces. I spent that time plotting my timing and exam execution, scribbling down some key points, references, solutions, and formulas I may need to use later.

The invigilator signals; it's time to begin the paper.

Inhale. Exhale. Relax!

I opened the exam paper, looked around, and saw everyone else rushing to answer the questions.

I could hear my lecturer's voice ringing in my head, "Don't rush, look at the wordings in the questions carefully, and take your time to answer them completely."

So, I calmly opened the paper, skimming through the entire exam sheet, highlighting question wordings, and plotting my answers to each question. I planned out, exactly, which questions to answer straight away or leave for later and how much time to spend on each question.

I remembered another important piece of exam advice given to me by lecturers and other academically strong students.

LESSON #2: IF YOU'RE BEING ASKED AN ESSAY TYPE QUESTION, EXAMINERS ARE LOOKING FOR YOUR INDIRECT, A.K.A. COMPLETE, ANSWER TO THE QUESTION

Initially, when I heard this advice at the start of the year, I thought it was really stupid. I still believed, at that time, the only information I needed to learn and use in exams was primarily from lecture notes and basic textbooks.

Later in the year, this made sense, because I had already spent a lot of time learning to deeply understand the course material from as many outside sources as possible. When asked on the spot to explain a concept, I could do so comfortably, clearly, and with my own "spin" on it. I never felt comfortable explaining the concept in a linear manner, since there was so much extra reading, journals, and other perspectives for tackling the problem I could introduce.

Later, I found out that this wider, independent, and indirect approach to tackling question problems was exactly how examiners separated the top students from the rest of the flock.

By "directly", a.k.a. incompletely, answering a question without expanding, the examiner may perceive that you only have basic understanding and only stuck to lecture or basic textbook material.

Applying all that I had learned, I managed to finish all my exams on time and left each exam knowing I put in my full effort. Yes, there were a couple that I felt I screwed up, but I said to myself, "I've done my best. I leave the rest in God's hands."

LESSON #3: YOUR EXAM RESULTS DO NOT DEFINE WHO YOU ARE AS A PERSON; WALK AWAY KNOWING YOU GAVE IT YOUR BEST AND LEAVE THE OUTCOME TO BE

In Part 2 (the extras) of this book, I will show you how to effectively revise for your exams, prepare for written essays and other important details leading up to exams.

RECAP:

- As you approach the end of the year and as exams approach, expect to see a lot of students panic, undergo stress, and throw around a lot of last minute information. If you've done your preparation, you don't have to follow the crowd. Just stay focused.

- Preparation for an exam is exactly that: It is preparation for an exam. Make sure to review past paper questions to get an indication of what to expect in the exam and practise taking the past paper exams in timed condition.

- All your hard work could go to waste if you screw up your exams. Make sure to take a deep breath, relax, look at the questions carefully, don't rush, and begin to write your answers at your own pace.

- Don't be afraid to show the examiner that you have done a lot of wider reading, extra research, and learning OUTSIDE. Typically, in essay type questions, the examiner is looking for you to demonstrate that you have deep understanding of the material, alongside independent thinking and "flair". This way, you avoid answering the question directly (incompletely).

- No matter the outcome, if you gave it your best shot, then leave the results to be. You've worked extremely hard to get to this point and finish, so you should be very proud of yourself.

LESSONS:

- **Lesson #1:** Don't let the last minute panic and nonsense throw you off your game.

- **Lesson #2:** If you're being asked an essay type question, examiners are looking for your indirect, a.k.a. complete, answer to the question.

- **Lesson #3:** Your exam results do not define who you are as a person; walk away knowing you gave it your best and leave the outcome to be.

CROSSING THE LINE: FINAL YEAR RESULTS AND THE END OF THE JOURNEY

I found myself in exactly the same position as I had found myself the year before. Results were finally out; after all my hard work, dedication and commitment, I was still left in limbo as to whether or not I had crossed the line.

It was exactly the same routine as a year earlier: I woke up at 9 am in the morning, had my breakfast, went to the gym, etc. This time, there was something very different.

I wasn't anxious or worried about my results. I had given up complete control over the outcome, and I knew I had given 100%. No matter the results, I knew I didn't let myself down and had no regrets, so I was relaxed and calm.

Once again, my parents were waiting downstairs to hear my results. Everyone in the family knew that it would require the miraculous for me to achieve those first class marks in final year. The odds were very slim.

I took a deep breath, opened my laptop, and logged into my student portal to see my results.

Page load ....1 .....2......3....4.....

What?!

Flashing right at the top, I saw I had averaged comfortable first class marks in my final year, even averaging over 80% in one of the course's hardest modules. Which meant I had achieved my dream: a 2.1 degree!

Words cannot explain that exact moment. I don't want to sound cliché, but it literally felt like I was dreaming or hallucinating. I had gone on this incredible journey to achieve this dream that was all an idea in my head. Even though I had put in a lot of work, I still had no idea how it was all going to come together.

That didn't matter at that moment. I felt relief, happiness, adrenaline; it was as if I had just won the gold medal in the 100m Olympic event.

I had made my parents and family proud, as well as the other people who had supported me – my friends, fellow students, and my tutors and lecturers. Most importantly, I had made myself proud, because I didn't let myself down.

Fast-forward to graduation day. I'm standing next in line to be called to collect my final year university degree. As I turn around and look through the crowd, I see every single person who had been involved at some point in my entire university journey.

I saw my parents smiling at me, overwhelmed with happiness, new and old friends from my university course, tutors and lecturers, students, and mentors who had been extremely helpful to me throughout the year.

Everybody involved in my incredible journey was watching. The ceremony master calls my name:

"Mayo Oshin, can you please step forward."

At that moment, I felt like I was walking up to a podium to collect a trophy. As I collected my degree, I pumped my fist in the air as the crowd stood up to applaud. Everybody in the auditorium acknowledged my achievement; a standing ovation followed.

The final push was over. I beat the odds and turned my graduation dreams to reality.

A Quick Recap
Below I have put together brief summaries and takeaways from each section of the book.

SECTION I

- Nobody cares about your excuses and why you didn't achieve the success you dreamed about; this is now all on you. Take full responsibility for your current and future situations, and take practical steps to make your dream a reality.

- Another crucial step towards your success is for you to begin with the end in mind. Create a clear vision in your mind and put some real emotion into it. Really see it, like it is real, and make sure to play out this vision as often as possible throughout the day. This vision will be your source of motivation, drive, and strength, especially during periods you feel like giving up.

SECTION II

HABIT 1: SEEK FIRST TO UNDERSTAND AND THEN BE UNDERSTOOD

- A solid understanding of your course material is crucial for your success. Examiners will give you higher marks if you show them you have a deep understanding with independent thinking.

- Practise "active recall" and continue to hunt for feedback from as many sources as possible. This will help you close gaps in your knowledge and deepen your understanding.

- Embrace "You. Only. Learn. Outside. (YOLO)". Look outside your lecture notes and textbooks and allow yourself to explore the real world to further expand your understanding of the course material.

- Make a decision to actively seek knowledge, put in the work, and you will find that the passion and curiosity to learn more will naturally increase.

- Give examiners exactly what they want; use the feedback they have given you to gauge this, or directly ask them what they expect. Once you understand what they want, you can deliver this in examined work and "be understood".

HABIT 2: SURROUND YOURSELF WITH PEOPLE THAT SUPPORT YOUR DREAM

- Final year is not the time to be proud and arrogant. Humble yourself and ask for help if you need it.

- Socialize and surround yourself with likeminded, sucess-driven students, and over time, you will find that their "can do" attitude will rub off on you.

- Understanding what the examiner is looking for is crucial for your success. So take the time to develop a personal and working relationship with them.

HABIT 3: TAKE CARE OF YOUR MIND, BODY, AND SPIRIT

- A healthy balance of the body and the soul positively reinforces your mind, which is the key for your success.

- A well-balanced spiritual life will give you the necessary peace of mind to keep you on the path to your dreams.

- Take good care of your body; this will give you the necessary energy you need for the long, tedious journey in final year.

HABIT 4: DON'T MANAGE TIME; "OWN" IT

- Forget time "management" of your to-do list; "own" and dominate it instead.

- Owning your time will give you more flexibility to prioritize, rank, and change your daily activities.

- Time is limited; it is also the most valuable resource you have available to you, so spend it wisely.

- By having a clear plan of action for your activities before the day begins, you can eliminate a lot of procrastination because you will feel a greater urge to cross the activities off your list.

SECTION III

Two radical and effective solutions for (P.A.D.S.) Panic, Anxiety, Depression, and Stress:

- Panic, Anxiety, Depression, and Stress are the top four emotional problems you may face. These can easily hold you back from achieving your desired goals, but there are simple strategies to minimize or overcome them.

- One solution to PADS is to minimize or eliminate bad sugars from your diet. Excessive intake of bad sugars will cause massive yo-yo swings in your hormonal levels and eventually your emotions. By reducing your intake of bad sugars, you rebalance your emotions and regain your clarity of mind. I have one very simple piece of advice to help you decide what food to eat: "If the food you are about to eat did not exist in a similar form 100 years ago and you do not understand some of the jargon on the ingredients label, then you're much safer not eating it."

- Another solution to PADS is fasting. Whether you decide to fast daily, bi-weekly, or monthly, fasting is a great way to detox your body, rebalance your emotions, and improve your energy and concentration levels.

Revision, Exams and all other Last Minute Nonsense

- As you approach the end of the year and as exams approach, expect to see a lot of students panic, undergo stress, and throw around a lot of last minute information. If you've done your preparation, you don't have to follow the crowd. Just keep focused.

- Preparation for an exam is exactly that: It is preparation for an exam. Make sure to review past paper questions to get an indication of what to expect in the exam and practise taking the past paper exams in timed conditions.

- All your hard work could go to waste if you screw up your exams. Make sure to take a deep breath, relax, look at the questions carefully, don't rush, and begin to write your answers at your own pace.

- Don't be afraid to show the examiner that you have done a lot of wider reading, extra research, and learning OUTSIDE. Typically, in essay type questions, the examiner is looking for you to demonstrate that you have deep understanding of the material, alongside independent thinking and "flair". This way, you avoid answering the question directly (incompletely).

- No matter the outcome, if you gave it your best shot, then leave the results to be. You've worked extremely hard to get to this point and finish, so you should be very proud of yourself.

LESSONS:

- **Lesson #1:**   Failure is only feedback: fail hard privately so you can have mega success publicly.

- **Lesson #2:** Y.O.L.O.
- **Lesson #3:** Pursue effort and the passion will follow.
- **Lesson #4:** It's not about you, so give the examiners exactly what they want.
- **Lesson #5:** Surround yourself with likeminded, success-driven students.
- **Lesson #6:** Develop a working relationship with tutors and lecturers.
- **Lesson #7:** A well-balanced spiritual life contributes significantly to your peace of mind.
- **Lesson #8:** Your body (health) is the main source of your energy.
- **Lesson #9:** Spend majority of your time on profitable activities.
- **Lesson #10:** Time is the most valuable resource you have, so invest it wisely.

PART 2
THE EXTRAS

STUDY ESSENTIALS AND STRATEGIES

This section of the book is an added bonus to the main book. I will be more in-depth in answering and solving frequently asked questions and problems you may face during the academic year. This includes writing first class essays, eliminating distractions, overcoming procrastination, and utilising revision strategies. Let's begin!

HOW TO OVERCOME PROCRASTINATION AND LACK OF MOTIVATION

Procrastination is by far one of the biggest problems you will experience as a student. It costs you a lot of time during the week that you can't get back, and ultimately, it holds you back from achieving your goals.

All that time you wasted that could have been spent studying, working, and learning cannot be recovered.

The worst part about all of this is the simple fact that procrastination sets you back on your work and now you are trying to meet tight deadlines that are causing you high levels of stress, anxiety, and panic. This is the worst state to be in because it negatively affects your academic performance and results. But, there is hope.

You may never be able to completely eliminate procrastination, but you can reduce it enough to become a lot more productive than you are right now and get a lot more work done. Before I share some strategies in overcoming procrastination, it's important that you first understand the root cause of your procrastination. This will require some time reflecting and observing patterns in your behaviour and thoughts. As you become more self aware of what is going on internally, you can begin to take steps to break free from this problem.

There are several potential reasons for your procrastination. You may be resisting doing the work now because you anticipate that it will be boring, difficult, or overwhelming. In other words, you anticipate pain from the task and would rather not have to face it now. This is why instead of working you'd rather watch YouTube videos and mess around on social media, as these things instantly give you pleasure with little or no pain involved. On a deeper level, you may resist the work now because you fear failure and rejection, possibly because you are a perfectionist and anything less than the best is unacceptable to you.

Research has shown that by procrastinating we are avoiding the negative feelings associated with working now (Pychyl, 2010). The twist here is that we ultimately end up feeling guilty and defeated after procrastinating.

Now that you have a clearer idea of what may be holding you back from taking action, we can examine some strategies to overcome your procrastination. I suggest you simply pick one of these and apply to your daily routine.

#1: BREAK DOWN YOUR BIG TASKS INTO BITE-SIZED TASKS

It's only natural to avoid facing a task that is big and intimidating, especially when you're attempting to complete the task in one session (McCrea et al., 2008). Big tasks are pushed forward till 'tomorrow' when we hope to feel more ready to take on the task. Unfortunately, this 'tomorrow' never comes.

Rather than give up on this task completely we can focus instead on the smaller steps leading to the accomplishment of the big task. So for example, if you need to finish writing a dissertation of 15,000 words, you can simply break down the task into small bits of 200 words per day. This amount is much less intimidating and easier to get on with.

The key lesson here is to shift your focus and attention away from the big mountain task towards the small bite-size steps instead.

#2: Take a very small baby step towards your goal

The main obstacle holding you back from taking massive action is simply that you're not taking any action. The truth is all you simply need to do is start doing something no matter how small and then the momentum will build until the task is completed.

Don't worry about the big task ahead, and simply ask yourself this one simple question:

'What is the smallest, easiest and most simple step I can take towards this goal right now?'

And then simply just do it! Forget about perfectionism, the pain and the struggle. All you're doing is taking a very small baby step and that's it. You can take all the pressure off yourself by knowing you don't have to tackle the entire task right now.

In the context of writing a dissertation, this could be as simple as writing the introduction. You will find that the momentum will build and you will automatically find yourself doing a lot more work than you anticipated.

#3: REWARD YOURSELF AFTER COMPLETING TASKS

If studying and working were fun and enjoyable, nobody will be procrastinating on it. But in reality, we get little or no pleasure, especially when the work is challenging, so we would rather not do the task right now.

Research has shown that we can break the habit of procrastination by introducing enticing rewards at the end of completing tasks. I would recommend that you reward yourself with something you consider to be fun, i.e., YouTube videos, Facebook, etc. Simply set a period of time where you will work without distractions and a period of time you will reward yourself afterwards.

These are some simple actionable strategies to eliminate procrastination from your study life. I suggest you pick one of these to help you. Most likely, your procrastination problem is deep-rooted, so spend some time in deep inner reflection so that you can shed light on the internal resistance keeping you in this trap.

A QUICK NOTE ON LACK OF MOTIVATION:

What do I do if I'm struggling to motivate myself to study?

Relying on the feeling of 'motivation' before you take action is a big mistake; after all, you brush your teeth every morning without actually feeling 'motivated' to do it. What we are trying to create here is the 'habit' of studying, so that you no longer have to rely on your feelings to take action.

Building new habits begins with self-awareness and introspection. I would like you to pay close attention to your study habits for a week, particularly pay attention to what 'triggers' you before you put off studying for something else. So for example, if you notice that the 'trigger' before you procrastinate is being in a study room with your friends, take note of that. Also, take note of how you feel afterwards; do you feel relieved from stress after putting off work? Take note of this as well.

By the end of the week you should begin to see a pattern emerging on what triggers you to put off studying, what you do instead of studying, and how you feel afterwards. As an example, you may have discovered that being in an environment with your friends around cause you to put off work and start joking with them. You may have also noted that this made you feel happier and more relaxed.

Now you can simply begin to experiment with changing your 'triggers', to create the new routine and habit of studying. In this case, one simple change would be to study in an environment where your friends are nowhere near to distract you. Once that's in place, simply set a dedicated time after working when you can joke and banter with your friends. This way, you get the same relaxed and happy feeling afterwards without compromising on your work.

In my own case, in my final year of University, I created a trigger of simply putting my headphones in my ears with instrumental hip hop music playing. Just like an athlete, I used the music to get me in the zone and ready to begin studying. You can do the same thing too and create the habit of studying.

SUMMARY:

Procrastination holds us back from achieving our goals because it wastes our valuable time on unimportant tasks that do not bring us closer to where we desire to be. The reason we procrastinate is most likely a deep-rooted internal problem, or it's a defence mechanism against perceived failure, pain, fear and stress. Taking time to reflect on and look for patterns in this internal dialogue is the first step to overcoming procrastination.

There are a couple actionable strategies we can take to overcome procrastination. These include breaking down your big tasks into bite-sized steps, taking a very small baby step, and rewarding yourself after completing a task.

Finally, in order to 'motivate' yourself to start studying and get more done, you have to shift your focus into building the habit of studying. The best way to build the studying habit is to become self-aware of what 'triggers' you to put off your work and change the 'triggers' to form the new healthy studying habits.

LECTURES: *HOW TO MAKE THE MOST OUT OF THEM*

Prior to my final year of University, my University lecture attendance hovered around the 50% region. It is no surprise that I later achieved marks that hovered around that same percentage. In my final year I adjusted to attending 90% of my lectures and my results skyrocketed. There is no coincidence here either.

Lectures are just one of those things in life that you have to learn to love. It's easy to resist the idea of attending lectures because you find the lectures boring, irrelevant, and unnecessary. I feel your pain, but lectures are a lot more valuable than you think.

One reason to attend lectures is that it cultivates strong discipline and work ethic. Think about it. If you can discipline yourself to attend 9 am lectures, you will be able to discipline yourself to work when you don't feel like it and get much more work done. Another plus is that you'll have a greater incentive to take better care of your health and sleep earlier, which will ultimately boost your energy levels.

Another great reason to attend lectures is to allow your subconscious mind to absorb and store important information for you. Even though you may feel like you're not learning anything during the lectures, the truth is your brain is doing a lot for you and it's storing all that information. Without being consciously aware, your brain may be helping you solve problems and fill in gaps of knowledge you may have. The best part about this is if you get stuck during the exams, you will be able to recall information that you were not even conscious of learning.

A final reason of attend lectures is simply the fact that you may miss out on very important information. Some lecturers are notorious for sharing crucial examination advice exclusively to students who have attended the lectures, and you don't want to miss out on this.

When it comes to getting the most out of lectures, preparation for lectures is crucial. Lectures are a reinforcement of your understanding of the topic, and likewise, it should help you identify gaps of knowledge you need to address after the lecture.

The worst thing you can do is to view lectures as your source of learning new information. You'd be much better off if you had pre-read the topic beforehand and walked into the lectures actively looking to reinforce this knowledge. This way you're not completely confused during the lecture.

Another benefit of pre-reading is that you'll have a much easier time keeping up with the pace of the lecturer and picking out the most crucial information.

Another way to maximise your experience at lectures is to change your sitting position. Where you sit down during the lecture can affect your level of concentration and attention to detail. The closer your seat is to the lecturer, the more likely you will feel less self-conscious to ask questions. You also concentrate better and pay more attention. I personally sat two rows from the front, but I advise you experiment and pick whatever sitting position works for you.

In the Note-Taking section of this part, I will share with you some effective strategies on how to take better notes during and after lectures.

SUMMARY:

Lecture attendance is much more important than you think. Lectures help you reinforce important ideas, cultivate self-discipline, and pick up on crucial information for your examinations. Pre-reading before your lectures will help you keep up with the pace of the lectures and further deepen your understanding of the topic. Changing your sitting position could also help you in improving your concentration and attention span during the lectures. Experiment and find what works for you.

NOTE-TAKING: *HOW TO EFFECTIVELY TAKE NOTES AND USE THEM WHILE STUDYING*

Note-taking is an essential skill for learning and studying your work, especially when you're in the process of deepening your understanding of course material. Research has shown that students who take lecture notes on average have better academic results (Kiewra, 1985).

You may feel like you don't need to take notes during lectures or when reading course textbooks. But, you will have a much stronger memory retention and deeper understanding of your course material, if you simply take the time to take notes by either writing on your notebook or typing on your laptop. You could even record lectures with your phone and listen for as many times as you want when you get home. Although, I will recommend writing on paper as research has shown that memory retention is better this way.

THE KEY TO EFFECTIVE NOTE TAKING IS SIFTING THE MOST IMPORTANT KEY POINTS FROM THE "NOISE".

The problem is that too many students waste too much time highlighting and writing notes on every single detail that they hear and read in the lectures and textbooks.

This approach is a waste of your precious time and reduces your ability to develop a deep understanding of your course material, which is required to score the highest marks.

So, how do you know the most important information to take notes on?

Effective note-taking begins with your end goal in mind. If you desire a first class degree, then you have to reverse-engineer the results you want, investigate and research what information you need to learn and understand, and then demonstrate this in your examined work so as to score first class marks.

So for example, if you discover that the examiners reward higher marks for use of credible journals and articles in your arguments, then you know that you should focus your note-taking on this. This will allow you to concentrate on what is important and stop wasting time on irrelevant note-taking.

This will be particularly useful during lectures. If you're continuously taking notes and listening, your multi-tasking will lead to confusion and reduced memory retention. But if you practise selective listening and only take notes on what is really important, then you will find that your focus, concentration, and understanding of the topic will increase.

During lectures, also pay particular attention to what the lecturer stresses as an important point. This will also be a strong indicator of what to take notes on. Particularly, if you have any gaps in knowledge on an important topic, pay attention during the lecture to take notes on the areas you are struggling to understand and follow up by speaking to the lecturer for further questions and clarification.

Once you're out of the lecture halls and taking notes from textbooks and other reading sources, the same rules apply:

FOCUS ON WHAT IS IMPORTANT

As you're reading the material, you should already begin to visualize and imagine what your final essay and examined written work will look like. Note-taking is simply a way to help you gather your "ammunition" and structure together. So as you read, ask yourself this simple question:

IS THE INFORMATION I'M READING CONTRIBUTING TO MY DESIRED FIRST CLASS MARKS?

If the answer is no, skip over that particular chapter and move on. The only material worth taking notes on are those that will directly be used in your final examined work to get you your desired marks.

Once you've started to hone what's important, you can now take notes. One particularly effective way of taking notes is to read key points supporting a particular argument (usually a couple of paragraphs) and afterwards re-write what you have read in your own words. This will help you focus your attention on important information and deepen your understanding. This is particularly useful when reading boring texts and complicated material. It will keep you engaged and help you concentrate better.

If you're taking notes of the work of another person's written work, make sure to take note of the author's name so that you can give credit to them and avoid plagiarism. Eventually, you should end up with well summarized and concise notes to which you can quickly refer months later (i.e. when revising for exams) to remind you of core key points on that particular topic or argument.

A QUICK TIP ON TAKING NOTES FROM CREDIBLE SOURCES
AND JOURNALS

If your course requires wide reading from journals and
written academic work, you should be familiar with
the long reading lists and the in-depth – and sometimes
boring – journals.

I made a major mistake early on during the first
term of my University semester. I watched other
students and copied what they were doing with
regards to taking notes from journals. They printed
out the journals, highlighted, and read through the
entire journal, taking hours to complete. After wasting
hours taking notes from journals and noticing that my
marked work wasn't getting better, I stepped back and
asked myself if there was a better way to do this.

I quickly realized that the only thing that matters
in the eyes of an examiner is that I could use the key
points of credible academic sources in the context of
my arguments. They didn't care about the details of
the journal itself as long as it was crucial and important
to the entire topic or course.

Once I understood this, I would simply read and
take notes of the synopsis at the start of the journal,
which summarized the key points of the journal. Then,
I would skim through the document all the way to the
conclusion, which summarized the key points as well.
After the notes were completed, I would consolidate
this under a particular category of arguments or key
points I would make in the examined work.

So for example, if I knew that in an exam I would
make an argument supporting freedom of speech and
the journal was about the importance of freedom of

speech, I would simply categorize my notes of that journal like this:

Arguments for freedom of speech
Mayo et al. (1992)

> *"They argue with evidence from a sample of 100 students in the University of Canada that freedom of speech...."*

Remember, note-taking is all about building ammunition for your final examined work, and luckily, I discovered early on how to prioritize my time and energy for this.

Using this method, I was able to storm through and take effective notes of each journal in under 10 minutes! This was a significant reduction in time compared to the hours I had wasted printing and highlighting irrelevant information.

This is why it is so important to start with the end in mind. If you have no idea what the examiner expects from you in order to get a first class, how will you know how to best allocate and prioritize your study time and note-taking? By coming to grips with the fact that "hard work" is not sufficient and prioritizing work is your key to success, you free yourself and begin to look at your academic work differently.

SUMMARY:

Effective note-taking can make or break your academic ambitions. Effective notes-taking will help you further improve your understanding and memory retention of your course material. Plus, they help you quickly remember important information, especially when you begin revision for examinations.

Effective note-taking begins with you being very clear on what you want to achieve and deconstructing what is required to get that. Once you have a clearer idea of what you need to take notes of, you can simply begin sifting the most important key points from the "noise". In the process of note-taking, you can practise writing what you've read in your own words to help you stay engaged and not get bored of reading.

DISTRACTIONS: *HOW TO GET RID OF DISTRACTIONS AND IMPROVE YOUR CONCENTRATION*

The rapid development of technology has made our lives faster, easier, and more efficient. But, it has also created a lot of distractions, especially when you're trying to study and work.

In the process of studying and taking notes, it's very easy to allow the distractions around us to take our focus off our work. Whether your phone is ringing or you get bored and check Facebook, distractions leave you getting very little work done and eventually getting behind in your work.

Unfortunately, there are no magic tricks to solve this, but there are some effective strategies you can try out. Just pick one and focus on it.

#1: ELIMINATE ALL FORMS OF DISTRACTION UNTIL YOUR WORK IS COMPLETED

This one is self-explanatory and simple, but extremely effective. I made sure during my final year of University to study and work in a distraction-free environment. Personally, I feel there are way too many distractions in the library, so I would work in the faculty buildings instead. I would also listen to non-distracting music that helped me concentrate on my work and block out external noise.

The biggest distractions in most cases are our phones and the internet. So, I'd strongly advise that you silence your phone and refuse to touch it until mid-day. The same rule applies to email and social media. This will leave a lot of time for you to study and get your most important work done first thing during the day.

Building this habit will most likely in a struggle for you, especially if you're addicted to technology. In the prior section on procrastination, I explained how you could build better study habits, so you can refer back to that for more details on how to build new study habits.

#2: PRACTISE SHORT BURSTS OF FOCUSED WORK

Simply change your perspective of working from "studying" to "sprinting". Sprints are intense and focused, but they are also short. The same approach can be applied to studying. Rather than block out straight hours to work on your tutorials or academic work, simply block out short "sprint" sessions of 20-30 minutes each. In between each sprint, you can rest for around 10 minutes.

Because the period of "sprinting" is so short, you will essentially be forcing yourself to focus and be alert. This is another effective way to eliminate distraction and stay focused.

#3: PRACTISE ACTIVE READING – USE YOUR HANDS

If you find yourself getting bored of studying, it becomes much harder to resist distractions. Let's be real here. Reading can be really boring, especially when there are a lot more interesting and entertaining things to watch online.

But, the truth is, studying in itself isn't "boring"; it's how you study that matters. Passive reading, without actively engaging yourself, will most likely bore you to tears.

So why not take a different approach? Whenever you're studying or taking notes, make use of your hands and engage yourself. Practise recalling the information you have read in your own words, use different colours as you take notes, and even draw diagrams to help remember key points.

Do whatever it takes to keep your work engaging and interesting. You will know what's best for your personality. If you like listening, why not record your voice summarizing the key points of the topic? If you're more visual, you could record yourself talking and even draw diagrams with pictures. Whatever style suits you, use it.

#4: BREATHE

Lacking self-discipline or self-control and allowing yourself to get distracted go hand in hand. If you can build your self-discipline, you won't allow yourself to be easily tempted any longer.

Research has shown that you can build your willpower and self-discipline by practicing intentional breathing and meditation. All you really need is five minutes of quiet meditation every day, and over time, you will find your willpower and self-discipline increasing.

SUMMARY:

Technology can be a big distraction from actually getting work done. Eliminating distractions and concentrating better begins with an intentional decision to rid your environment of any distractions until your studying is done.

You could also break down your studying into blocks of intense sprints as well as actively engaging yourself with the material.

If you find that you lack the self-discipline and self-control to avoid distractions, spend some time every day in quiet meditation and breathing. This will help your brain develop and build more "willpower".

HOW TO WRITE FIRST CLASS ESSAYS

Up until now, in Part Two, we've focused on getting the most out of lectures, effective note-taking, studying, and eliminating distractions. If your University course is heavy on the use of words instead of numbers, your ability to write brilliant and engaging essays could be the difference between achieving the first class marks you desire and failing to reach that goal.

In this section, I will show you the key essentials of writing first class essays. I applied these strategies to drastically improve from writing third class essays in my second year to writing first class essays in my final year of University.

Before we continue, you have to first make a decision that you will produce first class essays. Without this clear intention, you can't expect to magically stumble into a first class essay. Achieving a first class essay requires a completely different strategy and perspective from that of a 2.1. So by preparing your mind for this, you'll be able to push through the frustrating process and difficulties along the journey of polishing your essay writing skills.

Before we jump into the actual essay writing, let's explore some steps to help prepare you for success:

#1: PICK THE RIGHT QUESTIONS

Your examiners have given you a wide range of questions you can pick from for your essays. It's up to you to select the right questions that help you showcase your strengths and hide your weaknesses. The only way to determine if a particular essay question or topic is suitable for you is to do some investigation ahead of time. Speak to students in the year above, look at past papers, and talk to lecturers. Your job is to figure out exactly how much information and detail is required to score the highest marks for those questions or topics.

So for example, if you discover that a particular essay question or topic is intensive in diagrams alongside written content, you may decide to avoid this topic and focus on an essay topic that requires no diagrams.

By being strategic ahead of time with the topics and questions you tackle, you can already begin to prepare yourself to achieve first class marks.

#2: PAY CLOSE ATTENTION TO THE ESSAY QUESTION'S "TRIGGER WORDS"

Every essay question has trigger words that usually appear at the start of the question. These will help you gauge the type of answers the examiners are looking for.

Examples of trigger words are:

Assess, describe, compare, discuss, explain, state, outline and justify.

Each of these trigger words requires a different style and delivery of your essays. So for example, if a question begins with "discuss", straight away it's clear the examiner is looking for an essay that covers both sides of the argument, usually with extensive use of credible sources and journals to back up each key argument. Likewise, "analyse" may mean the examiner is asking you to make use of diagrams in the essay to strengthen your arguments.

I personally experienced that the further you progress in your academic years the more extensive "discuss" type questions will be required from you. Essentially, final year students will be required to deliver a "discuss" type of question in most cases.

Regardless, different examiners and institutions require different details for each of these trigger words. It's important that you speak to your lecturers to assess what they require from you.

#3: MAKE USE OF CREDIBLE ACADEMIC SOURCES IN YOUR ESSAYS

If writing essays were the equivalent of warfare and your arguments in the essay were your soldiers, then your use of sources to back up each argument would be the guns. Without the guns, you will lose the war because you're fighting with bare fists and no weapons.

By the time you reach final year, examiners will become much more ruthless in marking your work. Basically, what this means is that if in the first year of University you got away with scoring high marks in your essays with little or no use of academic sources, you will fail the same questions in final year if you answer them the same way.

The reason is that examiners expect that, as you progress through the academic years, your ability to analyse and write essays like a true academic should increase. That's why the use of these sources could be the make or break for your academic aspirations.

WHERE CAN I FIND THESE SOURCES?

Honestly, majority of these credible journals and sources have already been given to you in your reading list. Once you find one credible source, you can simply follow the rabbit trail and find many more, because they tend to cite and link to one another. The key here is to focus on sources that are deemed credible in the eyes of your lecturer as well as the general academic community regarding that particular topic.

So for example, let's say you discover whilst learning the topic of freedom of speech that there is a major case and article with respect to this topic. Additionally, this particular academic journal is constantly being referred to by your lecturer, the textbooks, and other journals as being a credible authority on answering that question. If you would answer a question on this topic and forget to include this case or journal in your written answer, you most likely won't get first class marks.

The reason is that the examiner will view your work as being "incomplete" and "unprofessional", because you have failed to identify and assess a very important piece of academic source.

You stand a much greater chance of achieving first class marks with the use of a few but significant academic sources than a lot of irrelevant academic sources. Quality, not quantity, is king in the land of academic referencing and sources.

How do I make use of these sources in my written essays?

Once you've sifted the quality sources from the rest, your guns are fully loaded and you're ready for academic warfare.

Firstly, I would encourage you to make use of the Harvard referencing style. This would usually look like this:

Mayo et al. (1992). How to write a first class essay. In: The Final Push, 1st ed.

In the context of a written essay, you could simply use this as a support for an argument:

> *"Making use of credible sources in a written essay is crucial for scoring first class marks. Mayo et al. (1992) argues that the quality of academic sources outweighs the quantity used within an essay. Furthermore...."*

This method of referencing academic sources will give you a lot more flexibility and room to focus on supporting your arguments effectively, thereby, achieving more marks.

The key to effectively using references in your essays is to look at your essay from the perspective of the examiner. They are sceptical about your arguments until proven otherwise, and you can provide credibility by making use of credible authors and academics in your work.

#4: STRUCTURE AND WRITE YOUR ESSAYS TO MAXIMIZE YOUR MARKS

Following on from my analogy of warfare, if you fail to plan, strategize, and execute in battle, you will lose. Likewise, poor structure, writing style, and execution of your written essays will significantly decrease your chances of achieving first class marks.

Before I show you how you should structure and write your essays, I'd like for us to pause at this point and stress a very important point that many students forget. The point is this:

YOU ARE WRITING FOR THE EXAMINER, SO GIVE THEM WHAT THEY WANT!

By simply embracing this one philosophy, you can save yourself wasted hours and achieve first class marks. When I was scoring third class essays, I wrote in a style that read well to me, structured in a way that suited me and essentially produced an essay that met my own standards. As soon I shifted my focus to writing to appeal to the examiner, my marks significantly improved to first class marks.

The more you can get into the minds of the examiners and discover what they really want to see in an essay, the higher your chances of getting first class marks. So, for this reason, I highly recommend that before writing any essay, you do some serious investigation about what is required to achieve first class essays.

Attend office hours and speak to lecturers, get your hands on the first class essays from current or past students, and analyse your own marked work. Look for patterns in the essays that do well and those that don't; are you using many unnecessary references or very few quality references? How long are the essays and how in-depth are they? What is the structure and writing style of the essays?

These are the types of questions that you will resolve by doing this investigation beforehand. Nothing I say here or you read elsewhere will reveal the "secret" formula of first class essays to you because every examiner and institution has its own requirements and standards of excellence.

You have to take the initiative and do in advance the research that most students are not willing to do because you want the first class marks that few students will ever achieve.

THE PERFECT STRUCTURE OF AN ESSAY

Sorry, I lied. There is no perfect structure, but there is a general structure that you can rely on in most cases. The structure goes like this:

Introduction:	*Addresses the main question with your main argument and outline for the rest of your essay.*
Body:	*Constructs supporting points and references for your main argument. Presents counter-points and references against your main argument.*
Conclusion:	*Summarises the key arguments of your essay with an independent constructive conclusion on the main question.*

I've kept it very simple because I know that too much detail will cause confusion. How you make use of this structure will be the make or break on whether you achieve first class marks or not. If you have done your homework and investigated exactly what your examiners want for a first class essay, you will already know exactly how to add flesh and style to this skeleton structure. This is more of an art than logic, and there are so many nuances to take into account: writing style, tone, flair, etc.

In my personal experience, the best structure and style for your essays will come directly from the written work of:

Your examiner.

Is it a coincidence that academics constantly refer to each other's work? No. The truth is: your lecturers and tutors are academic professionals. Outside of lecture halls, they are real human beings with aspirations for groundbreaking ideas, research, and outstanding contributions to academic journals.

In other words, those "extra reading" academic sources and journals are written by lecturers and examiners themselves!

The proof is in the pudding. All you need to do is emulate what you see. How do the academics begin their introduction to their essays? What is their style of writing and the "voice" of the writer? Begin to practise emulating what you read and watch your marks skyrocket.

Having said that, let's look at some general rules for addressing each section of essays.

INTRODUCTION:

The introduction is crucial to making a strong first impression and prepping the examiner to give you maximum marks. Imagine the examiner sitting at his desk with a cup of coffee in one hand and ready to fall asleep after marking over a dozen essays in the past 4 hours. It's the same old rehashed introductions and boring essays and he is about to call it a day. Then he reads the introduction of your essay. How will he respond?

If you do all of this right, your essay introduction should cause him to sit up, drop his cup of coffee, and literally grab your essay paper in both hands in anticipation of what will be coming next.

Your job during the introduction is to:

i. Show and demonstrate that you have read the essay question and the "trigger words" carefully.

ii. Provide a brief roadmap and structure of your essay.

iii. Clearly state your "thesis" (this is your main argument or case) that you will be evaluating during the essay and make it clear how you plan to do that.

iv. Be concise and engaging, and demonstrate a strong command of your use of language, i.e., style, tone, etc.

I don't have a working example for you here because I want you to actively do the homework and research I have previously outlined to discover what works best for your examiner and University. There's no point spoon-feeding you. I want you to succeed, so please take the time to do the investigative work.

BODY:

If you nailed your introduction, your examiner should already be engaged and eager to read what you have to say next. Your body is the meat of your work and will be heavily weighted towards your final mark.

The body of your essay should contain two essential elements:

- Supporting points and references for your main argument
- Counter-points and references against your main argument

The key here is to understand that for every point or argument you write, you must back it up with credible sources and examples. This will make sure your essays pass the "academic rigor" test.

The best mindset in approaching writing your essays is to imagine that you are having a one-on-one live discussion with your lecturers about the essay question. During the discussion, you want to converse with them at their level, as academics. Demonstrate that you have a strong understanding of the topic with knowledge of the key events, academic sources, and material, while maintaining your independent thinking and "swagger".

For every point, reference, and paragraph you write, the examiner is asking, "Why is this relevant to this question?" You have to be able to answer this question very effectively.

Also, make use of counter-points against your main arguments (thesis) to demonstrate that you have a well-rounded perspective of the topic and the ability to "evaluate" and "scrutinize" information.

So for example:

"Freedom of speech has been invaluable in the progression of our society. Through freedom of speech, women have been able to gain much more rights than they have been able to do before. However, Mayo et al. (1992) argues that women's rights were already in progress long before the introduction of freedom of speech in the modern society. Although, I will note that in coming to this conclusion Mayo et al. only studied one country and so the sample size for this conclusion is insufficient.

Additionally, Oshin et al. (2000), studying a much wider range of countries, discovered that there was a correlation between the rights of women and freedom of speech. Nevertheless, Oshin et al. (2000) suggested that this correlation wasn't completely due to freedom of speech but other environmental factors, i.e., political changes."

Did you notice something very odd about those two paragraphs?

My style of writing changed. I used words like "however" and "nevertheless". My use of referencing, i.e., Mayo et al. (1992), is used to support every single argument. And finally, I make use of counter-points, making a case against every point and evidence I use. In essence, I am continuously arguing back and forth with myself and challenging every case I make.

Pay close attention to academic journals and sources. You will find that they do the same thing. Don't try to reinvent the wheel. Learn from the best and emulate them.

Conclusion:

The purpose of your conclusion is to summarize the key arguments you wrote during the essays and make your own independent, constructive concluding statement to the main essay question.

Essentially, your conclusion should be brief and concise enough so that if someone didn't have time to read your essay but skipped to the conclusion, they would have a good idea of what your essay was all about.

Make sure that it's clear to the examiner that you have now come to a conclusion in your essay. It should be in an entirely separate paragraph and will usually begin with words like "in conclusion," "to round off," etc.

After your conclusion is complete make sure to go over your work and check for grammatical and spelling errors. You don't want to lose unnecessary marks on the basics, so make sure to spend some time doing this.

Writing timed exam essays

The same rules apply when writing exams in timed condition, except for the fact that you have a much shorter time to deliver your "speech" and get your point across.

The only reason why you will study well during term time and flunk your written exams is because you never prepared to write in timed condition. This is a very important mindset shift I want you to walk away with, because it could cost you your University degree.

Studying and working hard during the year is a necessary prerequisite, but wouldn't it also make sense to actually practise writing essays in similar conditions to the real exam?

Take time out to practise writing essays and answering past paper questions in timed condition. This will help prepare you mentally and also allow you to resolve any writing or timing issues you may have before entering the examination halls. As a plus, you can always hand over that written work to your lecturer to get more feedback on your progress.

Please don't skip over this step! It's heartbreaking to watch students, who worked very hard during the year, fail to reach their goals simply because of poor timed examination techniques. You don't have to experience this for yourself. Just do the preparatory work beforehand.

SUMMARY:

Writing first class essays is an art that takes a lot of time, dedication, and persistence to achieve. However, you can increase your likelihood of success by simply taking time to investigate what your examiner wants in your essay. By far, the fastest and most effective way to write first class essays is by observing and emulating the best works on your academic topic. You could retrieve the first class essays of other students, speak to lecturers for advice, study the writing style of academic sources, and improve on the feedback you get from your own written work. Just pick a method that works for you and stick to it until you're getting the results you want.

EXAM PREPARATION: *HOW TO EFFECTIVELY REVISE FOR EXAMS*

Before you begin revision and studying, it's very important that you have a clear strategy on how you plan to cover each unit and module in your course. The key here is to break down each module into mini-topics, sections, and key ideas so that you can revise each one individually.

Remember that the revision period is not a time to be learning new essential information. This should have been done during term time. The purpose of revision is to revisit, reinforce, and deepen your understanding of your core modules. It's an opportunity to quickly run a diagnosis to identify your gaps of knowledge, misinterpretations of information, and areas that need to be strengthened.

With this in mind, you can begin to lay out an effective revision timetable. During my final year, I created a revision timetable that allowed me to focus on a specific issue in each module every day. I revised two modules per day in blocks of 30 minutes for a total of 5 hours.

When you create your revision timetable, ensure you do not underestimate how much time revising each module will take. The most important thing is to focus on the topics and issues you're struggling with early on in your revision schedule before addressing where you are already strong.

Personally, I had completed revision of all my modules five weeks before the exams began. By the time I resumed at the University for my final term, my only focus was refining, mastering, and deepening my core understanding of the topics. This gave me enough time to ask important questions and receive crucial feedback before my examinations started. Also, it took a lot of pressure off me because I knew that stress, confusion, and panic would ruin my chances of getting first class marks.

When revising, use past papers to help you identify what areas of that topic you should be focusing your time and energy.

Past papers generally are a poor indication of the 'exact' questions that will show up in the exam, so if you try and predict the exact examination questions, you'd be heading towards disaster. The secret to using past papers is not to focus on the question but the information the question is trying to extract from the examined student. Think about it. There are several combinations of questions I may ask you to get you to give me answers to why you want first class marks. It's not the questions that matter; it's the quality of your answers and the information used that matter. With that in mind, focus on finding patterns in past paper questions that try to extract certain information from you. This will give you a good indication of where your revision focus should be on.

You can get even more strategic, especially if you're taking exams for modules that give you a choice of written essays to pick from each topic in the module, i.e., pick 3 from 6. Clearly in this case it's inefficient to study all topics painstakingly because you won't have enough time or energy to do that.

If you've done your past paper investigation properly and you have a fair idea of the details required to get a first class in that topic, you can begin to narrow down to four topics you will specialise in. Honestly, if you have a strong understanding of three topics, the fourth can simply be a backup. By taking this approach, you can further prioritize your study time effectively.

Now that you've prioritized your revision topics and have a schedule, it's time to actually study and revise. The most effective method of revision I have found is to simply get a blank sheet of paper and write the most important ideas of the module in one page. This will really force you to focus on the key concepts and will be a source of quick reference when you're approaching exams. Then I would get another blank page and try my best to recall each topic in my own words. Whenever I got stuck, I would simply refer back to my one page and notes I took during the semester. I repeated this over and over for each topic within each module until it was close to perfection.

If you are writing essays in your exams, take some time out to practise timed essay writing. I wrote in detail about this in the 'writing first class essays' section of this chapter.

When you return back to University from holidays, you should have a couple of weeks before examinations. This is your opportunity to go to office hours to ask lecturers for answers to problems you struggled with during revision. You can also take these practice timed essays to the lecturers and tutors for their feedback to see if you're on track for a first class. You can even begin to teach and help other struggling students as well because this will further help you in understanding your modules, as well as highlighting what you need to work on.

It's now time for you to take your examinations.

SUMMARY:

The revision period is not a time to be learning new and important information; this should have been done during term time. The purpose of revision is to revisit, reinforce, and deepen your understanding of your core modules. It's an opportunity to quickly run a diagnosis to identify your gaps of knowledge, misinterpretations of information, and areas that need to be strengthened. With this in mind, you can begin to lay out an effective revision timetable by breaking down your modules into mini-topics that address the most important sections of your module. Tackle the difficult and most important topics early on in your revision plan before the easier, less important topics. Refine and master your knowledge by asking for feedback from lecturers, asking questions, and teaching other students.

BONUS: *FINDING AND GETTING A JOB*

First off, I'm not a career or job advisor, so this part of the book shouldn't be taken as gospel. I'd advise you speak to someone who is an expert in this area for advice.

Make sure to join the student email list. Simply send your name and email to **mijooear@gmail.com** and you will be sent information and tools to help you get a job after graduation.

There are two situations you may find yourself in, as you prepare to land yourself a job. Either you are applying for jobs mid-way through the term time or you're applying for jobs after you graduate from University.

If you're applying for jobs during the academic year, managing your time will be crucial. Balancing and staying on top of your academic work with job applications can be extremely stressful and difficult. The most important thing here is to break down your daily tasks to only 3 most important things you need to accomplish and forget everything else no matter what.

Likewise, prioritize your job application process. Do you really need to send job applications to sixty companies? This kind of approach will (1) reduce the quality of your job applications, (2) waste your energy and time, and (3) damage your self-confidence.

The truth is you have a lot of value to potentially offer to any company, so why not approach your job application with this same mindset. Limit your job application process to a handful of companies worth your time and energy. Don't limit yourself to the well-known companies; there are smaller boutique firms that will provide quality training and support for you as well.

Keep your working days very simple and try your best, if possible, to complete your job applications in the first term of the academic year. This will help you free more time to focus on your academic work.

When applying for jobs, it's important to put yourself in the shoes of the employer. They are looking to hire the best talent that will give them a return for their investment. In other words, they are looking for leadership potential in every applicant.

One way employers sift through applicants is by looking for relevant work experience. The Graduate Market Survey of 2011 discovered that out of some 17,500 graduate vacancies, nearly a third (5,600 positions) were to be held for students who had prior work experience with the employer. When asked about the likelihood of a student with no work experience being hired, 60 per cent of employers in the survey responded that it was either not very likely or not at all likely (High Fliers Research, 2011). If you get the opportunity to intern at an organisation or get some experience in a similar job, your odds of employment will be higher than otherwise.

Another way that employers filter candidates is by looking for constructive events in your life where you have demonstrated leadership. For example, if you have led, promoted, and organized a charity event for the homeless kids, you can clearly use this to demonstrate and highlight your ability to lead and make things happen. It will also show the employers that you have the basic skills to be a good employee, i.e., communication skills, problem-solving abilities, etc.

Even with the best preparation, your job applications may still get turned down. Don't lose heart. Understand that this is a numbers game and simply try and get as much feedback from each application and interview on what to do better in the next one. Eventually you will land yourself a job and begin your professional life.

CONCLUDING REMARKS

First off, I would like to congratulate you for completing this book. I understand you're already under a lot of pressure to read your university books, so to take time out to read this book completely is truly a blessing. Well done!

If you got this far and have already started to apply some of the concepts I mentioned in this book, you will be well on your way to achieving your academic dreams and the first class marks you desire.

Remember, at the end of the day, you can only give your best. Your self-worth and future success in life has no direct relation to your academic achievement in final year. As patronizing as this may sound, try to enjoy the journey, because you will never be able to get your university experiences back. Give it your all, take care of yourself, enjoy the journey, and let go of the outcome.

If you got any value from this book, share it with other University students who will need to know about the information in the book. I truly hope that someone who was in the same situation as myself will achieve first class marks because of this book.

At the end of this book, you will find a bonus section that contains step-by-step worksheets to help you take action on the concepts in this book.

Whatever unique strategy, plan of action, or method you decide to use in your journey is completely up to you. You know yourself best, so keep experimenting and find what works for you.

I hope this book was useful to you, and I wish you the best of luck with your results.

Finally, I look forward to hearing your success story. I truly hope that you have an experience much more inspirational than mine.

Take care,

Mayo

PART 3: APPENDIX

References

Blansky, D., Kavanaugh, C., Boothroyd, C., Benson, B., Gallagher, J., Endress, J. and Sayama, H. (2013). Spread of Academic Success in a High School Social Network. *PLoS ONE*, 8(2), p.e55944.

Duhigg, C. (2012). *The power of habit*. New York: Random House.

Fond, G., Macgregor, A., Leboyer, M. and Michalsen, A. (2013). Fasting in mood disorders: neurobiology and effectiveness. A review of the literature. *Psychiatry Research*, 209(3), pp.253-258.

HECSU, (2011). *What Do Graduates Do?* 2011. What Do Graduates Do?. [online] Manchester: HECSU. Available at: http://www.hecsu.ac.uk/assets/assets/documents/WDGD_Nov_2011.pdf [Accessed Dec. 2011].

Hershner, S. and Chervin, R. (2014). Causes and consequences of sleepiness among college students. *Nature and Science of Sleep*, p.73.

High Fliers Research, (2010). *The Graduate Market In 2010*. The Graduate Market. [online] London: High Fliers Research Limited. Available at: http://www.highfliers.co.uk/download/GMReport2010.pdf [Accessed Oct. 2011].

High Fliers Research, (2011). *The Graduate Market In 2011*. The Graduate Market. [online] London: High Fliers Research Limited. Available at: http://www.highfliers.co.uk/download/GMReport11.pdf [Accessed Oct. 2011].

Kapler, I., Weston, T. and Wiseheart, M. (2015). Spacing in a simulated undergraduate classroom: Long-term benefits for factual and higher-level learning. *Learning and Instruction*, 36, pp.38-45.

Karpicke, J. and Roediger, H. (2008). The Critical Importance of Retrieval for Learning. *Science*, 319(5865), pp.966-968.

Kiewra, K.A. (1985). Providing the instructor's notes: An effective addition to student note taking. Educational Psychologist, 20, 33-39. McCrea, S., Liberman, N., Trope, Y. and Sherman, S. (2008). Construal Level and Procrastination. *Psychological Science*, 19(12), pp.1308-1314.

McGonigal, K. (2012). *The willpower instinct*. New York: Avery.

Peet, M. (2004). International variations in the outcome of schizophrenia and the prevalence of depression in relation to national dietary practices: an ecological analysis. *The British Journal of Psychiatry*, 184(5), pp.404-408.

Pychyl, 2010 The Procrastinator's Digest: A Concise Guide to Solving the Procrastination Puzzle.

Bonus Section

First off, make sure to join the student email list. Simply send your name and email to **mijooear@gmail.com** and you will be sent information and tools to help you get first class marks and land your dream job.

INTRO

In this free section you will find some valuable tools that will help you make the most out of this book so that you can achieve first class marks. It's important to break down massive goals into tiny little steps that will build momentum over time. This is the purpose of these worksheets below which have been assigned to the applicable sections of this book.

Please make sure you read the applicable sections in the book before diving into the worksheets. I also advise you take your time working through these; a lot of these steps are habits that will take time to develop.

Be patient with yourself and take it one step at a time. In fact, to avoid getting overwhelmed, you can simply pick one part of the worksheet to work on every month and don't worry about the rest.

CONTENTS

Worksheets:

Section I

Step 2:   Begin with the end in mind

Section II

Habit 1:   Seek first to understand and then be understood

Habit 2:   Surround yourself with people who support your dream

Habit 3:   Take care of your Mind, Body and Spirit

Habit 4:   Don't manage time; "OWN" it

Transcript on how to stop procrastinating and take action right now!

SECTION I

STEP 2: BEGIN WITH THE END IN MIND

In this section of the book, I mentioned the importance of having a clear vision for your final university dream degree. This will be a massive boost of motivation and drive to succeed. I also walked you through my personal vision as an example for you.

NOW IT'S YOUR TURN TO CREATE YOUR OWN VISION:

In the blank space below I would like you to write out your own vision. Look through the eyes of your future self, living in that dream.

Here are some questions that will help you write this:

- What do you see?
- How do you feel?
- What university degree are you holding?
- Who is around you on graduation day?
- What does results day look like, and how do people react around you?

Really describe and be detailed about exactly how you "feel" as if it were real for you right now. Don't worry about it being realistic or whether there are grammatical errors, etc. It's only a fantasy, so just let it all flow out.

Just focus on the feeling.

Write down your vision below:

Once you're done, I'd like you to sit or lie down in a comfortable position and quiet surrounding, close your eyes, and replay the scenes you just wrote down about your vision. If it helps, play some music and spend a couple of minutes deeply breathing to relax before you begin the exercise.

Set your timer for only 5 minutes and dive into your imagination.

Remember that replaying this vision daily will help you develop a solid self-belief and drive in achieving your dream. The daily habit is much more important than the amount of time you spend in one session, so just focus on this for only 5 minutes everyday.

SECTION II

HABIT 1: SEEK FIRST TO UNDERSTAND AND THEN BE UNDERSTOOD

Under this habit, I discussed the importance of first understanding your academic material and your examiners, and then being understood by them when you hand in examined work. To develop this habit, we first have to practise how to effectively "understand". Write down your answers in the spaces below:

1. What beliefs are holding you back from pursuing "understanding" instead of memorising? (i.e. you believe it will stress you out, it is too much work, etc.)

2. Using the blank space below, write down in the centre a topic you're currently struggling to learn. Brainstorm and write everything you can remember about this topic, including examples, references, drawings, etc. Stop when you've run out of ideas.

3. Most likely you have gaps in your knowledge from #2. Now let's practise Y.O.L.O. (You Only Learn Outside). Using the blank space below, in the centre write down YOLO. Brainstorm and write anything, anywhere, or anybody you can reach to gain the necessary knowledge to complete #2 perfectly. (Here are some ideas: YouTube, seminars, workshops, journals, speaking to lecturers, etc.)

4. Select the top 5 credible sources that suit your learning style. Simply use 1 credible source this week to close your knowledge gaps. At the end of the week, repeat the exercise in #2.

5. When you repeated the exercise, did you struggle to recall the most important information? If so, use your next best credible source that suits your learning style. Keep repeating this process until you're almost perfect in brainstorming that topic.

BONUS:

Remember when I mentioned how my student mentor, Olga, was reinforcing her understanding by teaching me concepts I didn't understand. You can do the same thing here. You don't have to restrict yourself to brainstorming on a piece of paper. Why not try and explain the topic to other students and get them to challenge you with questions?

We can take it even further. To truly understand something means that you are able to explain that concept or topic in the most simple and basic form whilst getting your point across clearly and originally.

One way to practise this is the 'eight year-old' test. In other words, if you can explain that topic simply and clearly to an eight-year-old or anybody who has no prior knowledge of that topic, then that's a strong indication that you now have a strong grasp and deep understanding of that topic.

6. Find someone who has no knowledge of the topic you are learning and tell them that you would like to to them. Tell them they should ask questions if they don't understand. If you struggle to clearly explain the topic or respond to their questions, then you have to go back to your "sources" to learn more.

7. Now that you have gone over the exercises a couple of times, go back to read your answers in #1. Do your beliefs hold up to your experience of pursuing understanding? Is it as hard or as boring as you thought? If your beliefs haven't changed, assess what you can change in your approach to learning to make it more enjoyable, e.g. listening to audio books instead of reading books.

HABIT 2: SURROUND YOURSELF WITH PEOPLE THAT SUPPORT YOUR DREAM

In habit 2, I highlighted the fact that you cannot achieve your dreams on your own. By surrounding yourself with like-minded, success-driven students and tutors or lecturers who are willing to support you, you will further reinforce your self-belief and be kept accountable to successful thinking and actions.

If you're introverted and socially awkward, this may be a bit of a challenge for you, because it may require that you step out of your comfort zone to speak to people you don't know. Don't let your fears hold you back from your dreams. This decision alone could be the difference for you.

Write down your answers in the spaces below:

1. Close your eyes and think of a person on your course who would be great to learn from and hang around. Take note of the first name or names that pop in your mind. What is the worst thing that could happen if you speak to that person or those people who could possibly be part of your dream team to support you towards achieving your dream?

2. What would be the worst thing that could happen to you from NOT stepping out of your comfort zone and reaching out to these students or teachers? (We already know the answer to this.)

3. Between #1 and #2, which outcome scares you the most or has the greatest consequences? (Hint: your answer should be #2)

4. Use your fear of #2 to drive you to step outside your comfort zone and interact with like-minded students. If you're still struggling with fear, ask yourself what you can do to add value to that individual or group. By focusing on adding value and helping instead of asking for help, your anxiety should reduce.

5. Repeat steps #1 - #4 with regards to your lecturers and tutors. They are human beings just like you, so take the time to interact with them.

Habit 3: Take care of your Mind, Body, and Spirit

In habit 3, I highlighted the link between your mind, body, and spirit, and specifically how they can positively or negatively reinforce one another. Your mind is at the core of your belief system, your actions, and your success. Your body will give you the energy to pursue your goals, and finally, your spiritual life is your source of peace.

There's no need to go overboard with this, so let's keep it really simple:

1. Off the top of your head, what would be your own personal source of spirituality? This could be prayer, meditation, going on a quiet walk, etc. Simply choose one and commit to practicing this for only 5 minutes everyday. Set a timer on your phone and stop when the alarm goes off.

2. What are your current sleeping habits? Do you wake up on time for your daily activities and feel rested, or do you sleep really late and wake up feeling really tired? Whatever the case, you already know what is best for you. If you're

struggling to discipline yourself to sleep earlier, simply make a commitment to sleeping half an hour earlier only once a week. Every week, you can adjust, little by little, how early you sleep until you reach your goal.

3. In Section III, I addressed the problems of PADS (panic, anxiety, depression and stress) and how changing your diet can significantly help reduce these. I said, "If the food you are about to eat did not exist in a similar form 100 years ago and you do not understand some of the jargon on the ingredients label, then you're much safer not eating it." I want you to write down everything you are currently eating or drinking on a regular basis that fits this description. There's no need to take extreme measures to eliminate all of these in one go. This will be too difficult. Simply pick one or two of these and replace them with the healthy alternative. For example, if I drink a can of coke for lunch, I would simply replace that with water or orange juice. Make a commitment to stick to these changes for only 30 days. After the 30 days, take note of how you feel in terms of your energy levels. Now you can replace two other unhealthy foods for another 30 days. Repeat the cycle.

Your current food and drink list:

Your healthy alternative for one or two of these:

How do you feel after 30 days and what is the impact on your academic productivity?

4. You don't have to go to the gym or work out 5 days a week to keep fit, energetic, and healthy. Off the top of your head, what would be a fun exercise activity that you could do in under 30 minutes? Once you have noted this, just go out and have fun exercising for only 2-3 times a week. That's only an hour and a half every week. Not bad.

Your 30-minute fun workout:

Your report on how you feel after the workout:

Your 30-day report on how the workouts have affected your academic productivity?

HABIT 4: DON'T MANAGE TIME; "OWN" IT

Under habit 4, I mentioned how I wasted time with unproductive "to-do lists" and how these gave me little flexibility to use my time properly. Time is the most valuable resource you have, so don't waste it on unproductive activities.

I introduced an effective way to "own" time in such a way that you can have more flexibility, prioritize your tasks much better, and readjust them freely if needed. Below I will walk you through the exact steps you can take to do this for yourself.

STEP 1: PLAN WEEKLY

Rather than planning daily, plan for your entire week instead. Remember that every "major" task is like a mountain to climb. By breaking down different sections of the mountain to climb, you are able to climb the mountain much quicker and more efficiently than otherwise. So for example, it would be more efficient to plan to write 7,000 words for your assignment, broken down into daily chunks of 1,000 words, rather than attempt to write 7,000 words all in one day.

By planning weekly, you can see the big picture of your major tasks and use each day as a tool to break down those major tasks or goals.

So, write down your plans for the week following my example in the book. Focus on the most important activities that you wish you to accomplish, as well as daily tasks, e.g. going for a jog, etc.

Step 2: Categorize your plans and activities

We need a way to differentiate what is really important and what isn't.

Okay, so let's take this to-do list and "own" it. Reorder the list, assigning:

- Urgent activities (U): These are the most important activities that need to be addressed as soon as possible.

- Important activities (I): These are also important activities but do not have to be addressed immediately and are not as important as the urgent activities.

- Uncategorized (no symbol is assigned for this): These are activities that would fall at the bottom of the list in terms of priority and urgency. So, typically, these events may be urgent but definitely not important, for example, a friend telling you to call them back as soon as possible because they have some gossip for you.

Use my example in the section for more guidance on how to do this.

STEP 3: RANKING THE ACTIVITIES AND PLANS

Okay, so you should have categorised your plans and activities. The key now is to rank them in order of most urgent and important all the way down to least urgent and important.
Let's do this:

STEP 4: NOW ALL YOU HAVE TO DO IS LOOK AT YOUR WEEKLY CALENDAR AND BLOCK OUT TIME FOR YOUR MOST IMPORTANT AND URGENT PLANS FIRST!

For example, you might decide that the best time to get started on your dissertation is Monday night. This way you have committed to your dissertation above any other plans that pop up Monday night.

I understand that this topic goes much deeper than this. Procrastination is a real problem and sometimes there are deeper issues like fear and peer pressure that affect our productivity.

HOW TO STOP PROCRASTINATING

5 SIMPLE STEPS I USED TO OVERCOMEPROCRASTINATION(TRANSCRIPT)

So you want to know how to stop procrastinating?

I know the beast of procrastination is real, but there is hope. I want to share with you 5 simple steps I have personally and successfully used to overcome procrastination.

Recently, using these steps, I have been able to write and publish my book THE FINAL PUSH in only 30 days, finishing the first draft of 17,000 words in the first two weeks alone. I was also working a full-time job and was able to maintain my sanity and health. All through that period, I also created two websites, this one included.

I don't say all of this to brag, but to inspire you to believe and take action to stop procrastinating.

We can never really completely stop procrastination, myself included. In fact, I confess I procrastinated a bit when writing this because I was focused too much on making it perfect.

What I can say is that by applying these steps you can drastically reduce your amount of procrastination and begin to take massive steps towards your goals and dreams.

Oh, and yes, you are not procrastinating by reading this

because you are learning how to stop procrastinating. You ready?

So why exactly are you procrastinating?

Relax, I know you want me to jump straight into the action steps, but let's step back for a minute. In order to defeat the beast, we have to understand the beast.

Know. Your. Enemy.

Scientific research has shown time and time again that the reason we procrastinate isn't because we are born this way. It's because the short-term benefits of procrastinating outweigh the long-term benefits of not procrastinating.

In other words:
Procrastination is simply your natural reaction to avoid pain.

This is perfectly normal so no need to beat yourself up over this. By simply understanding the fact that it is perfectly normal for you to avoid pain and suffering, you can begin to create an effective strategy to overcome procrastination.

Think about it.
If you can simply take away the pain or suffering associated with taking action on that goal, plan, or activity, then you would do it!

That's why we don't procrastinate when it comes to

doing things that bring instant pleasure and enjoyment. Watching a TV show to catch up on the drama, gossiping with our friends on the phone, and looking at pictures on Instagram gives us more pleasure than the pain associated with writing your dissertation or going to the gym.

So you already know how to NOT procrastinate. It's just a matter of training your mind to NOT procrastinate when it comes to your goals. So as you can see, it's not really about tactics; it's more about shifting your mindset and your perception of those goals and tasks ahead.

Alright, let's get into the steps.

STEP #1: STOP THE NEGATIVE SELF-TALK AND EXCUSES

- "I can't stop procrastinating."
- "I just don't have enough time."
- "Every time I try to work, I struggle to overcome procrastination. I can't help myself."

This kind of negative self talk and excuses are only going to hold you back from taking action.

Think about someone you know who is always complaining about being in a toxic relationship. She keeps saying, "I just can't find someone who would treat me right. I keep attracting bad, toxic men."

Okay, but the last time I introduced you to a really nice guy who would treat you right, you brushed him off for the dangerous looking guy who ended up treating you like crap.

Why would she continue to put herself in a situation she later regrets?

The reason for this self-sabotage is because she is simply taking action to reinforce her belief system. This is the exact process with procrastination.

The more you tell yourself that you "can't stop procrastinating" and keep making excuses, the more your actions will self-sabotage your efforts to stop procrastinating.

This is why this is a crucial first step, because nothing I share with you will work if you have already wired your mind to believe that you can't overcome procrastination.

It will take a while to completely rewire your mind and change your thinking habits, but there are simple steps we can take right now to build gradually towards that.

TRY IT: For the next couple of days all you have to do is simply catch yourself thinking or saying these negative thoughts and then replace them with the positive alternatives.

So for example:

- "I can't stop procrastinating when it comes to exercising," becomes "I can stop procrastinating. In fact, today I spent 5 minutes going for a run."

- "I should have written 2,000 words today. I messed up," becomes "It's okay. I'm only human. Tomorrow I will take the first step by writing 300 words."

You feel me, though. Practice this consciously a couple times a day for the next 30 days, and before you know it, your thoughts about procrastination will automatically be more positive.

STEP #2: IDENTIFY THE ROOT CORE BELIEFS THAT ARE HOLDING YOU BACK FROM TAKING ACTION AND CHALLENGE THEM

Fear, peer pressure, worry, anxiety, pain or pleasure, distractions.

Building on from Step #1, another effective strategy I have personally used is to find the exact beliefs I have that are holding me back from taking action and challenge them.

So for example, when writing my book, THE FINAL PUSH, I struggled with the fear of failure and putting myself out there to market the book. This fear held me back from taking certain actions that were in line with my goals.

So what did I do?

I simply wrote out all my beliefs concerning my fear.

- I am afraid that if I promote this book people will judge, criticize, and reject me.

- I am afraid that no one will buy the book and it will be a flop.

Then I challenged these beliefs by first asking the question, "What will I lose out on if I don't do this?" For me, this was the fact that:

- Someone, whose life could have been radically changed by reading the book, would never see it because I never promoted the book to them.

- If I don't take action, I won't be able to be a source of inspiration to other people who are struggling with the same fears.

As soon as I weighted the benefits and costs of procrastinating and letting fear hold me back from taking action, I realised that I am much better off taking action. This helped me to push through the fear and my procrastination.

My root cause of procrastination here was driven by fear of failure. What about you? Is it peer pressure, worry, distractions? Or maybe you just don't really care that much about that goal.

Whatever the case, by identifying the root core beliefs holding you back from taking action, you can challenge and eliminate them.

TRY IT: Simply write down your beliefs surrounding why you feel you can't stop procrastinating when it comes to that specific goal. So for example, if you want to start an online business, maybe you have the belief that it would be very expensive and ruin your entire social life.

Next, write next to this the costs of not taking action towards this goal. Really focus on the feelings of disappointment, self-defeat, etc.

Weighing both of them, hopefully the benefits of taking action should be much clearer to you.

Now ask yourself this question, "What simple step can I take right now to challenge these beliefs I have?" So for example, in the case of starting an online business being very expensive, you could simply type on Google, "How to start an online business cheaply." Then read articles about this and challenge your beliefs.

STEP #3: BUILD MOMENTUM BY BREAKING DOWN THAT INTIMIDATING TASK INTO THE MOST SIMPLE AND BASIC ACTION STEPS

If there's one thing everyone can agree on, it would be that:

A parked car isn't moving anywhere; it's going to stay exactly where it is.

In other words, you're just like a parked car if you aren't taking any action at all. It is better to do something, no matter how small and irrelevant, than to do nothing at all, because that momentum will continue to build until you're taking full action, just like driving that car at full speed.

The problem is most times we are facing a huge task or a goal, and we forget to live in the moment and focus too much on the mountain ahead. This intimidation and the potential pain we associate with taking action will keep "our cars parked". In my case, I knew I wanted to write over 15,000 words for my book, which was very intimidating initially. It's very difficult to take action and build momentum from this place.

So I simply broke down the 15,000-word mountain into a daily word count goal of approximately 1,000 words. Already you can see this target seems a lot more realistic, less painful, and easier to take action on. Everyday, I focused on that 1,000-word goal and not the 15,000 words. Eventually, I realised after two weeks that I had completed the 15,000 word count.

Maybe 1,000 words is too much for you to write daily.

No problem.

The point is to break down that goal or activity into such small, basic, and simple steps that you would have no problem taking action on them RIGHT NOW.

One effective trick I have been using lately is the 5-minute rule:

What I do is that I ask myself what simple step I can take right now and get done in less than 5 minutes? So if my plan was to lose 5 kg a month, my simple step would be to go for a 5-minute jog or walk.

The reason this is so effective is that naturally once we start doing something and it's enjoyable or easy, we want to continue that task and spend more time doing it.

Soon your 5-minute jog becomes 10 minutes and then 20 minutes, etc.

You've built momentum to accomplish the task by simply taking one basic step. So remember:

> *"Faith is taking the first step even when you don't see the whole staircase."*
> **-Martin Luther King**

TRY IT: What is the most basic, simple, and practical step you can take RIGHT NOW to accomplish your goal or task? Whatever that is, simply block out 5 minutes on a timer to do it. Once the timer rings, stop! If you feel an itch to continue the task, simply walk away for a few minutes break and then return for another 5-minute sprint.

If you can easily do this consistently for a week, simply raise the amount of time spent "sprinting". So instead of 5 minutes, you can spend 10 minutes instead. You can also increase your number of sets. So if you want to spend 1 hour on a task, you can break that down to six sets of 10-minute sprints with 5-minute breaks in-between the sprints.

STEP #4: SCARE YOURSELF TO TAKE ACTION BY CREATING URGENCY AND DEADLINES

We are emotional creatures, and generally, we love drama. Whether it's watching sports, movies, or TV shows, the emotional rollercoaster keeps us hooked.

Why not create some drama to help you stop procrastinating?

The reason I was able to complete 15,000+ words of my book in 2 weeks was because

DRUM ROLL................

I set a 2-week deadline to complete 15,000+ words of my book.

Simple, I know.

You would be surprised how much you can get done when you have a sense of urgency and a deadline approaching. You've seen this in action if you waited till the last minute to study for exams; your productivity shot through the roof.

The famous British historian and author, Parkinson introduced the idea of the Parkinson's Law in the mid-1950's. Parkinson's law simply states that:

"Work expands to fill the time available for its completion."

All this means is that if you give yourself two weeks to complete a two-hour task, then the task will become tedious and more difficult to complete than if you gave yourself less time to complete.

So inject some drama into your activities. You could set a weekly deadline or even a daily deadline. As long as it creates a sense of urgency and emotional incentive to take action, do it.

By setting a 2-week deadline to finish the first draft of my book, I had an extra boost of adrenaline and urgency pushing me. I was extremely focused whenever I was writing because I knew I had very little time to complete my goal.

TRY IT: Whatever goal or task you have, challenge yourself to complete it in half the time you initially set out to complete it. The point isn't to perfectly meet this deadline – most likely you will miss it – but the point is to create drama and urgency that will force you to take massive action.

STEP #5: REVERSE-PROCRASTINATE AND REWARD YOURSELF

Yes, you heard me. I'm asking you to procrastinate.

But in REVERSE.

What do I mean?

At any given time slot, let's say 11 am to 12 pm, there will always be two or more activities or plans fighting for your time. In my case, it was a fight between writing 1,000 words of my book or watching videos on YouTube. It's not always possible to fill in all of them. The aim is to complete the most important tasks first, then the least important later.

So check this out:

Even if I decide to write 1,000 words of my book in that time slot, technically I'm still procrastinating on watching videos on YouTube.

So either way, I am still procrastinating even though one task is more important than the other.

This is another trick I used to trick my mind to take action.

I simply told myself I was going to procrastinate on the task that was least important and then rewarded myself afterwards by doing that task.

I call this REVERSE PROCRASTINATION.

I procrastinated on watching YouTube videos so I could write 1,000 words of my book and then rewarded myself afterwards by watching YouTube videos.

This was extremely effective for me because I always knew that there would be pleasure at the end of my 1,000 words of writing. Not only that, but pleasure from the activity that would have wasted my time.

Remember in the intro, I mentioned how naturally, as humans, we avoid pain and run to instant pleasure.

The 1,000 words of writing didn't bring pleasure to me until I finished the entire book. So rather than wait till then, I simply gave myself instant pleasure after completing my task, with the activity I would usually have wasted time doing.

TRY IT: Off the top of your head, what do you usually procrastinate with? (i.e. watching TV, video games, etc.) You don't have to give these up, just reverse-procrastinate. Simply plan to do that activity after you've completed your important task to reward yourself.

END OF BONUS SECTION

ABOUT THE AUTHOR

Hi, I'm Mayo Oshin, the author of The Final Push. I'm also an alumnus of the University of Bristol where I studied B.Sc Economics.

Alongside my professional work as an insurance broker, I'm an entrepreneur, author, speaker, and pastime guitarist. My passion is inspiring and empowering the future leaders of my generation to be more productive, perform at the highest level in everything they do and live healthier, more fulfilling lives.

I'm not necessarily more intelligent, self-confident, or better than anyone. I believe that every single human being on the planet has the potential to experience and live an extraordinary life on the next level. This is what drives me to do what I do.

You can contact me at mijooear@gmail.com.

Mayo

Printed in Great
Britain
by Amazon